2011 WRITING FROM INLANDIA

Work of the Inlandia
Creative Writing Workshops

AN INLANDIA INSTITUTE PUBLICATION

2011 WRITING FROM INLANDIA
Work of the Inlandia Creative Writing Workshops

This publication is the end result of a three-season run of Inlandia Creative Writing Workshops held in three locations: Idyllwild, led by Jean Waggoner; Palm Springs, led by Maureen Alsop; and Riverside, led by Ruth Nolan.

The Creative Writing Workshops are part of the Inlandia Institute's Literary Professional Development Program, which also includes seminars on publishing and copyright. The purpose of this core program is to foster creative writing and support the emerging writers of Inland Southern California.

The Creative Writing Workshops began in Riverside the summer months of 2008. In addition to the Riverside, Idyllwild, and Palm Springs workshops, a workshop in Ontario has just been established, led by Cati Porter. All of these workshops support the rich literary talent that abides in this creatively vital region.

Workshop participants, many of whose works appear in this collection, are diverse in age, gender, culture, and writing experience. The writing samples here are from those who made it to the finish line with completed stories, essays and poems.

i

APPRECIATION

2011 Writing From Inlandia is an exciting realization of the Inlandia Institute's vision of an inclusive and collaborative enterprise that promotes writers with a regional voice and that stimulates a greater awareness of the area's diverse literary, artistic, and cultural heritage. This new annual anthology would not have been possible without the vision, energy, generosity, support, and outright hard work of many talented people.

When *Inlandia: A Literary Journey Through California's Inland Empire* was launched in 2006, people asked if that were all; what about the new emerging authors. We were most fortunate that Ruth Nolan responded by starting the first Inlandia Creative Writing Workshop in Riverside, and for *Slouching Towards Mt. Rubidoux*, the chapbook she created to celebrate the work of the emerging talent in that group.

Jean Waggoner and Maureen Alsop followed suit, forming and leading workshops in Idyllwild and Palm Springs that nurtured the talent in those unique places. Their skillful mentoring tripled the writing productivity of workshop participants and challenged the institute to effectively present it. We embraced that challenge. It propelled us into developing an annual anthology of *Writing From Inlandia*.

All aspects of producing this first anthology, under the Inlandia Institute's own imprint, fell to the dedicated and talented volunteers on the Inlandia Institute's Publications Committee: Maureen Alsop, Ph.D., Gayle Brandeis, Julianna Cruz, Judy Kronenfeld, Ph.D., Ruth Nolan, Jo Scott-Coe, and Jean Waggoner, chaired by the multi-talented and energetic Cati Porter. They did it all. We may be word people, but words of sufficient gratitude fail us here.

Special thanks also to graphic designer Julie Frenznick for visually interpreting the "regional voice of Inlandia" in the cover design of the anthology, which evokes the complexity of our culturally rich and diverse region, and will brand this new work as *Writing From Inlandia* for years to come.

Thank you, too, to the writers who put themselves forward to write about this place and to tell their stories. Thank you for your courage, and for sharing and trusting us with your words.

Finally, thank you, Poets & Writers, for supporting the Inlandia Creative Writing Workshops through a grant from the James Irvine Foundation.

-Marion Mitchell Wilson, Executive Director of the Inlandia Institute

2011 WRITING FROM INLANDIA

Work of the Inlandia
Creative Writing Workshops

TABLE OF CONTENTS

SURVEYORS OF TIME

INLANDIA CREATIVE WRITING WORKSHOP - IDYLLWILD
LED BY JEAN WAGGONER

CONTRIBUTORS

Myra Dutton - David Calvin Gogerty - Emily Heebner
Don Lenik - Joan Koerper - R. M. Mozeleski
Christina Lee Nordella - Joy Sikorski - Jean Waggoner

The Heinrich Maneuver

Heinrich, though virtually indistinguishable from a flesh and blood human being, was an android, designed by a team of Caltech scientists to penetrate uninhabitable corners of the universe. Given his first opportunity to prove himself, Heinrich was sent to Hawaii's constantly erupting volcano, Kilauea, to distill vital essences from the source of creation itself. His mission, one that had puzzled alchemists for hundreds of years, was to bottle the elixir of life, this time, however, via computer, into thousands of stacked trays of water vials.

Heinrich, whose electrical synapses were built to withstand the greatest extremes of cold and heat, understood that entering the cauldron of an active volcano was within his capacity as a Model 3000 Robot Explorer, his exterior impervious to even the greatest meteoric impact. However, perhaps due to the hypersensitivity of his brilliant creators or simply a defect in the newly developed titanium wiring that held him together, Heinrich felt he was on the verge of a meltdown, fueled by the critical expectations of his task.

No matter how hard he tried to analyze it, Heinrich remained extremely vulnerable and distraught, with no one to discuss his dilemma. Cyborg psychiatrists did not exist. His Caltech creators, new gods in the scientific community, had no clue that Heinrich might soon be frozen in his tracks due to an accelerated form of stage fright.

What should I do? Heinrich questioned the Universe, but the Universe did not reply. He could still hear the Board of Directors for Global Concerns—their aged, lined faces explaining why the world, especially now in the state that it was in, needed to keep its leaders healthy and strong. Heinrich's water of youth would not be offered to the disposable poor, they smugly informed him, indeed not, for this project had been funded by the wealthy power elite and was intended for their benefit alone.

The more Heinrich thought about it, the more he recognized that his uneasiness, at least partially anyway, originated from the people who controlled him. Heinrich began to devise a plan as he traversed Kilauea's summit caldera. Not only did volcanoes represent life and the timeless birth of islands and continents but they also offered instant death. If he allowed even the slightest amount of toxic gases into the vials, the recipients would find their power and influence suddenly coming to an end.

In Heinrich's version of a better world, this new mission seemed quite reasonable and effective. It only required a slight twist in his electrical wiring. This, he realized, was why he had been created. This and this alone would be his destiny as the world's first android anarchist: to eliminate corruption by single-handedly taking down the powers that be in order to begin the world anew. He could see the headlines now, as he began to reverse the procedure of filling the vials from a positive to a negative input—or rather, from the elixir of life to the elixir of death. *Heinrich the hero*, they would hail him. *Heinrich the savior of the human race*, they would shout as they hoisted his 500 pounds on top of their shoulders.

So involved was he in his devious plans, that Heinrich never noticed the open shaft, immediately before him, that extended 3000 kilometers deep into the core of the Earth, and with one more step, he vanished, never to be seen or heard from again. Caltech scientists mourned his loss, but soon replaced Heinrich with a newer model: the Henrietta 6000, which was far more compliant and advanced than any robot ever conceived before.

Ghost in the Rock

The rising half-moon
provokes lofty,
silhouetted celluloid images.
Ethereal etchings;
Incense Cedar garbed
in woven whorls of four.
California Black Oak
wearing bright green
six-lobed leaves.
Pointed bundles
of three-hundred year old
Ponderosa Pines.
Swaying portraits
jettisoned against
a midnight blue starlit sky,
rhythmically
shadow dancing
across the spongy
San Jacinto Mountain
forest carpet;
needles, acorns,
pinion pine nuts.
Flickering lights
in San Gorgonio Pass
imitate celestial luminosity
six-thousand feet below.

Spinning
   d
      o
         w
            n
the mountain
past Idyllwild,
maneuvering
a serpentine left turn,

the car beams
suddenly *illuminate*
a stark, white, looming,
granite outcrop
materializing to our right.

The jutting,
massive, canopied
                c
           l
           a
                w
primordial apparition;
sculptured rockwaterfall.
Magnetic;
demanding attention
and awe.
We gasp in unison.
Mesmerized
through the switchback
swerving now to our right
Ancient Beings
beckon us
into an invisible
archway of unity.
Are the Far Away Ones calling?
Those powerful,
flying mortals from outer space
who claimed this
sacred landscape
long before the Cahuilla people?

Or, Tahquitz,
with his legendary,
insatiable appetite
for human flesh?
Holding our breath,
veering back again
left,
we drive on.

The Coat

"Here," Mother said, thrusting her three-quarter length winter coat at me with an outstretched arm. "I can't stand the sight of it anymore. It's yours." Mother's sudden disdain for the coat arose when her abusive boss purchased the identical garment. Paradoxically, Mom's impulsive bequest helped save a young woman's life one sinister, stormy night.

I was thrilled with the coat. A heavy black woolen blend with leather loop toggles that slipped over elongated vertical wooden barrel buttons, it had a leather drawstring waist and an ample hood. Soft, white, furry luxurious lining trimmed the coat. The color contrast popped.

The ticker-tape strip at the bottom of the television screen was broadcasting warnings when the National Weather Service's trademark buzzing, mimicking a garish, insistent, 1930s doorbell, bellowed forth preceding the announcement. A massive winter storm front was swiftly moving across mid-central Michigan from the West. Home from Michigan State for my weekend visit, I had to get back to campus that night in time for early morning classes. Throwing on my coat, I ran out the door. I was heading straight into the blizzard.

The full brunt of the storm engulfed me on the expressway; Highway 96, two lanes in either direction separated by a spacious stretch of low-lying meridian. Beyond the road's shoulder, the embankment sloped away on both sides. The windshield wipers grappled against the deluge of sleet while the highway was rapidly turning into a solid sheet of ice sending my brand new 1969 lime green, three-on-the-floor, Chevy Nova into dizzying gyrations disregarding the studded snow tires. It had been over five minutes since I had seen another car.

I was well past Howell and figured I couldn't be too far from Weberville when I caught a glimpse of something desperately out of order, well off the road, near the tree line to my right. Don't even ask me how I saw it through the whiteout, but there it was. Slowly I reined the car to a stop and backed up. Getting as close to the edge of the road as I dared, engaging the emergency flashers, I left the headlights on and the car running. Fetching a flashlight from the glove compartment, I headed off toward the dark mass.

Night and blinding snow do querulous things with the imagination. It couldn't be, I thought. But, it was. My beam picked up the form. A body lay on the ground about six feet from an overturned, crumpled heap of a car that had nosedived into a tree. Blotches of red scattered on white gave the illusion of a surreal Jackson Pollack painting. In another few steps I saw it was a female.

6

"Hello? Hello?" I said clearly, approaching with caution. "My name is Mary Joan. I am here to help. I'm coming closer, okay?" No response. Taking off my gloves, I felt for the warmth of her breath, found it, and lowered myself on one knee. "You are going to be all right," I said. Motionless, she let out a soft moan.

Looking about my age, her slight 5'3" frame was splayed in an unnatural fashion. Her coat, torn open and crumpled between her torso and right arm revealed lightweight dress slacks. Already partially buried in a blanket of snow, her shoes were missing and her head was fully exposed to the elements. "I'm going to leave you for a few minutes," I said. "You will be fine. Help is on the way. Hang on." I started to leave and then turned back. First lowering the hood, I removed my coat, carefully placing it on top of her. Quickly checking the wreck to make sure no one else was trapped inside, I found a sweater and shaped it into a make-shift cap pillowing her head.

My ski jacket was in the trunk of the car, where I always carried extra clothes, gloves, and a shovel. Bundling up, I grabbed a hat and scarf, and headed for the middle of the highway praying for help. Minutes passed before I spotted barely visible headlights crawling toward me in the distance. Jumping up and down, waving my arms and flashlight, I began calling out for the vehicle to stop; it did. The nice couple, eager to assist, promised to call for an ambulance at the next exit.

Retracing my steps, I found the young lady unconscious. Offering words and gestures of comfort, I periodically brushed the accumulated snow off the coat and tucked it closer around her. When aid arrived, the ambulance driver asked if I wanted the blood-laden garment back. "No," I replied. The stretchers' buckles clicked shut over the coat. We left the scene in parade fashion; ambulance first, me, then the police.

At the hospital, I stayed just long enough to see the young lady reunited with her parents, capturing one last glimpse of a dangling, blood-stained toggle as the privacy curtain was pulled around the gurney.

P.O. Box

People in this mountain town don't get the mail delivered to their door, or even to their gate. The terrain is too rough for mail trucks. Sometimes we're snowed or iced in. Too many cabins are way back in the woods. So, there's no street side mail delivery.

What we have are Boxes at the Post Office. Small, medium and large. Patrons have their own keys, and whether walking or driving, they can pick up the mail every day, but on Sunday no packages can be picked up. For some it's a necessity; for others it's almost a ritual.

Inside, to the left, are double doors and counters. To the right the boxes are lined up and numbered, shoulder-high, in an L shaped wall that allows access to box holders. The boxes back up to a corridor that is closed off, where they are loaded by the P.O. employees. The whole thing reminds me of the food "Auto-Mat" of yesteryear, with little swinging doors, only now for mail!

And the small and medium sizes are see-through! Funny enough, they are also hear-through, as my wife and I found out one pickup day. We opened the box. I had trouble pulling out various items crammed inside, dropped some, and cursed mildly. And I heard a soft voice say "Temper-temper".

I ducked down and looked inside for the source of the voice. I listened. Silence.

I turned to my wife and whispered, "Did you hear that, my P.O. box admonished me!"

She said "Um, soooo?"

Then the 'Temper-temper' voice pronounced, "I am the Universal Conscience of all P.O. Boxes!"

At which my wife and I dropped everything, clutching at each other, and laughing helplessly, feeling a little dippy.

When I could catch my breath, I said, "Hey, we've found the funniest show in town". From behind the wall came "I'm happy if you're happy. Sometimes I have fun like this", (then in falsetto), "Help help, I'm stuck in here and I can't get out".

At this point, a man and a little girl had walked up. The man's mouth was agape, his key held in a hand that faltered. They had heard just the end of the plaintive 'stuck' appeal, and the girl, whining, with lips trembling, was pointing worriedly up at the boxes.

I bent again to near the opening and said, "Psst, you've got some people scared, they don't get the joke".

The 'conscience voice' said "Oh-what", (then in falsetto),

"It's OK, I got out, I'll be fine."

The man sighed, wagged his head slowly, and used his key. The girl hid behind his thick legs, then for a moment peeked around to see if anyone was looking.

My wife and I recovered our things, walked out, got in the pick-up, and drove for about a minute. Then, from laughing so hard, I had to pull over or wreck the truck. I had a stitch in my side. I was hurting, Sheila was crying for happiness; we consoled each other.

If you frequent this Post Office, you'll eventually meet everybody in town. Every time we go back, one of us fingers the key into the slot; we get the mail, and we always LISTEN. You never know when the 'Universal Conscience' is going to Strike Again!

9

French Fries Lizzy

We were eating at a table outside the deli in our town, when on the ground I saw a half-filled, discarded take-out pack of French fries. And it moved!

Nibbling on the fries was a little spraddle-legged camouflage green lizard. He-it was in reptile heaven! I had seen it, or one like it many times; sunning itself on a rock, or skittering out of sight as I appeared; the flicker of something moving out of the corner of my eye, somewhere in the garden.

If you have any land around here, this shy thing is a regular nine months of the year tenant. This creature blends in so well that, if it doesn't move, you won't notice. Works the other way too. If you don't move, it won't notice!

The cute, road crossing, bushy tailed squirrel is the village mascot; otherwise I'm sure the lizard would be so honored. I don't know the scientific book name for this tiny leftover from the age of dinosaurs; but when it crosses my path, I call it the FRENCH FRIES LIZZY.

Mummy

Fashions change, but a mummy stays a mummy forever! As a kid, one of the fist flicks I ever saw featured a mummy. In a re-run on T.V. last night, there it was again!

As usual, it walks, grabs, terrifies, mystifies; there's no end to its capabilities.

Brains removed, it has a mind of its own. This decidedly dead thing has a major score to settle, needs vindication, has a method, a plan; and modern weapons do not prevail against him; and it's always him, a BIG him! I guess a female mummy would be inappropriate film-wise, there's no cleavage in a linen wrap; but I would rather have Nefertiti in any kind of garb, than the best, scariest male mummy that ever lived, or died and returned again, still, yet, already!

Why Do Writers Write?

It's 98 outside, not a breeze within a mile. The little redhead is at it again, out there on that old hoop; that thing wouldn't know a level if it were getting whacked by one.

The kid is turning to a beet, his fair skin a gift from his French-Irish mom.

He's writing a play, working his lines with his imaginary brothers, (Budda & Gudda). They're playing against the new kid, "Kobe". Is he all that? Not today. The redhead with brothers in tow, are ruling the asphalt, same as yesterday, I'm sure tomorrow.

Why do writers write? Why does the redhead go back tomorrow? He takes a piece of something born once upon a time in his heart, he could tell you the day and time. Like a writer, a love flows in and out of him, moving on his court, his paper, writing his story. His untied shoe lace flopping around as he spins and twirls in his boyish world, dreaming his new play, his new story.

The writer looks out of the window, his young boy playing and dreaming effortlessly. The writer ponders the paper, blank, the pen tapping slowly. "How does that kid write so easy? Do his dreams have no end? That well is deep", says to himself.

And he ponders... Two hours go by and he's awakened by the new breeze blowing in the window, bringing an idea with it. His "ball" begins a dribble as if all by its self. A love story from his past rewinds, the sweet times bring a smile. The pen is moving on its own, recalling, reliving. Hours pass, emotionally drained, the sun is going down. A peaceful smile falls on his face. The love in his heart has been shared with, if nobody else, this paper, this court, dancing on it with graceful moves, imagining a different time, rewritten, edited and made perfect. Life's struggles for a moment given the back seat and a story given the wheel to a Sunday drive, eyes closed- smile on. The writer stops, love shared, peace made, at least with himself.

He looks out the window; the redhead is weary, hands filthy, clothes soaked. He goes to the fridge, gets lemonade and goes outside to see what his little redhead has written today; they look at each other, the answer apparent.

Diane

Through an open window
Where no curtain hung

Her perfume drifted in
To wake me from a dream

Her dark hair blowing in the breeze,
Though I couldn't see

Clear in my imagination
Bring my smile to full grace

My eyes are closed, I can see her lips
They're perfect in every way

Her eyes green, paralyze every man
But a quiet smile can bring peace to your life

Through an open window
Where no curtain hung
I see my love before me
My life "again"
Has just begun

Tears of a World

The world stopped today
The earth stopped today
(just) not in Japan

Their world's stopped
As if by shock, as if in shock
Their earth has not stopped
Their ground moving like a ship at sea

Their world's stopped
Neighborhoods, villages, towns just gone
A wave of mud, cleansing the earth of lifetimes and history
Entire families with no one to know
They've even vanished

Nature's version of holocaust

A hardworking people, struggling from decades of comeback
An ironic history, proud and not proud
Revisited again, not from war, but from nature

A paralyzed world looking on with disbelief with its own problems,
So heavy, but unlike this

Sobering

The world has stopped, taking pause
Restless nations struggling with their shackles
The world has stopped today and paused
Standing still in shock, sad, dismayed

We'll look numbly at the video file
Sad countenance and tears
There will be no smiles

We'll pick up and go on like September 12th
A resilience learned in a hard way

Hope is like a far way star
The light at the end of the tunnel
Lately seems to be an on coming train

Our human race, tossed in tragedy
Its future uncertain, to say the least

The Good Book says this all will pass,
But for today, for many, not soon enough.

Then I Looked at the Stars

Marionettes in the sky
With no care beneath His eye
The stars they hang, effortlessly floating
They're on time, every night
Surely just to humor Him
Simply to amaze us
A clock, a watch like no man's seen
Wheels and gears turning to perfection
My life a turmoil, all its parts
Like atoms bouncing off the walls
My worry never resting
How will I do this, Can I do that?
Feeling like a king staring at a bishop at my flank
Life's endless challenge, do you ever arrive?
My faith whittled to a limp twig
Sitting on the ledge, to tired to climb
I look down, I can't go back
Suspended in time, helpless in this moment
Darkness is setting in
Then I looked at the stars, on time tonight
Not one is missing
Who does this, He does this
Perfectly every night, His effort, non-existent
His power so great
My life so little, why do I worry
He pushes those stars without a hurry
Maybe if I stop fighting, sit down and relax
Stop running ahead and pushing back
Maybe like these stars, I'll have no worry
My problems are His, I need not flurry
Yes, I looked at the stars, so great and so grand
My problems, my worries
They look like sand

Blackbirds

The blackbirds had arrived,
You were trying not to notice,
along with the slow ticking of the clock,
above the water boiling on the stove.
Your grandmother had taught you,
the symbols and meanings
alive in your deeper nature,
but you fought it every time,
the awareness of a death coming.
That's when you'd start to make the tea,
calling to the spirits for miracles.
You never could remember.
You'll still try to read the leaves in the cup,
stirring you into a panic of anxiety,
the knowing pulling at you,
like a weed in your heart,
you thought you'd killed a thousand times,
tears in your eyes,
snow in your soul.
That's just when it comes,
the miracle,
as you place the hot cup down,
and let go.

Death

It was part of the womb you developed in,
nursemaid to those leaving
and Doula to those staying.
In truth it lives directly in the breathe,
surrounds our hearts with the thinnest of veils,
envelops our minds with fear.
Once you become aware,
you have the power of denial,
an exhausting method for life.
It will slip through your hands
while you work the day into night and then day again,
always just at the tip of your fingers,
turning into your desire to reach for things,
both inside and outside your soul,
knowing no inside or out.
Bulging with its own sweet milk
for the birth of itself.

Nightfall

Bare,
moonless,
lost in the rain
of your hair
gently falling,
the night fleshing out,
still waning
before dawn
and the goodbye coming.
A star,
wished into flight,
and surrender,
becoming prayer,
even forgiveness,
still wafting in the air,
the scent of sandalwood,
behind your knee
inspiring the dark
to just let go.
Breath so warm
against my neck,
stickiness,
licked up like honey
dew,
accumulating drops of time,
accounting for the heaviness,
in my heart,
that's been washed,
away

Stellar Peanut Success

Almost every day in the California mountain community where I live, Stellar's Jays flock around my patio area and either squawk to let me know it is time for their daily dose of raw peanuts, or one lone bird will land on top of my patio wall, perching as close as possible to the sliding glass door that leads outside, cocking his head and peering through the *mostly* clean glass to see if he can make eye contact with me. When he does, I laugh and slide the door open and toss peanuts onto the cement patio floor while talking to him like a cherished friend. He shrieks in delight to his fellow jays, "Peanuts, get your peanuts here!" like a hawker at a baseball game, then hops down nonchalantly to stuff one or two nuts into his bill. These brilliantly blue-colored birds bring much joy to my solitary life. They also teach me about success.

On one particular morning after I toss a handful of peanuts outside, I sit down on my living room couch to watch the jays snatch up the free food.

The first bird swoops down and lands a few steps from where I sit. The sliding glass door provides me with a direct view that does not distress the bird, so I watch as she effortlessly hops to a small peanut with a single nutmeat in it, pecks open the shell and instantly deposits the red-skinned morsel into her mouth. Without hesitating, she hops to another peanut, the largest one with three nutmeats in it; and I smile, inwardly cheering her uninterrupted focus as she picks it up with her sharp beak before flying off.

Fearless and smart, she knows how to arrive early when an opportunity presents itself and take whatever she wants with practically no effort at all, and without hurting anyone. She is the best of Ms. Biz.

Next, three other jays fly down. Each one hastily chooses a peanut, then flies away. Three wise guys, they follow the successful example of Ms. Biz and are on their way up the corporate ladder. They also happen to make a good Greek Chorus for another bird who later lands among the peanuts.

But now comes a single jay. At least five peanuts remain on the ground, easy pickings for her, but she seems afraid of some hidden or imagined menace. After she lands, she hesitates, keeps her head low and her feathers down as if something will pop out, attack her and take all the peanuts. An internal dialogue of "lions and tigers and bears, oh my" seems to control her antics.

She simply *cannot* decide whether or not to take a peanut. Afraid of making a mistake, she turns this way and that, watching, listening, suspicious, doubtful. She reminds me of myself many years ago and I am certain her name is Lily McClellan.

While she fusses and frets, Ms. Biz returns for a second course, ignores her and easily lands in the midst of the remaining nuts, where she quickly chooses the best one and flies off.

Even after seeing that there is absolutely no danger, Lily MClellan still takes no peanut. Instead, she seems more sure than ever that internally peeping "lions and tigers and bears, oh my" will somehow solve her problem, whatever that may be.

Meanwhile, a blustery boaster lands in an oak tree nearest the peanuts and makes sure all the other jays know who is the boss jay in this part of the forest. He jabbers loudly about nothing at all, but his chest puffs out with every booming squawk. He too turns this way and that, but unlike our fearful little bird, Big Bill is supremely confident and the other birds seem to come to attention when he speaks. He reminds me of my former husband.

After a few more moments of making his boisterous announcements, he pauses for a slight instant to gauge his audience, in this case the Greek Chorus, all three of whom have flown to the branches of a nearby apple tree to get a better view of the action. They chitter softly to one another, commenting on the wonderful Big Bill and what he might do for them. At this point, I realize that one of the three wise guys is actually a female. She seems mesmerized by Big Bill and reminds me of my former best friend.

Satisfied with their attentiveness, Big Bill makes a grand descent, lands a foot or two away from Lily McClellan, and continues squawking, only more intimidatingly now.

This forces a decision on Lily, but instead of taking a peanut, she allows Big Bill to chase her away. The Greek Chorus, especially the female, nods and chirps in amused approval.

Lily McClellan is a fool soon parted from her peanuts, hesitating in fear until an imaginary menace becomes a reality. She is a marketer's dream come true, the ideal consumer, jilted spouse or…the average voter.

Big Bill, now more confident than ever, continues to engage his captive audience. A squirrel watches nervously from a towering pine that stands a short distance behind the self-important orator. He too, would like the peanuts.

Big Bill ignores the squirrel, preferring to keep the other jays in his line of vision, especially the female who seems to titter when he looks at her. Naturally, this spurs him on to greater bravado while he turns to the left and turns to the right as though standing before two TelePrompTers, bragging to his spellbound audience in the apple tree.

In one brief moment, however, Ms. Biz, caring nothing for Big Bill's pompous proclamations or the Greek Chorus' prattling, stealthily lands behind the overstuffed bird, snatches up another peanut, then zooms off.

Big Bill, now a bit embarrassed and suddenly silent, sheepishly turns away from his audience. Not looking back to see what they think, he hastily picks up the second to the last of the peanuts and takes off a little less grandly than he landed. The female follows him to take advantage of his bruised ego. She knows how to get *his* peanuts.

Big Bill. Another fool. With a bit of coaching, he could become a mighty politician. Somehow, they always manage to take the little birds' peanuts.

Now Lily McClellan decides to try again. She lands near the last peanut but continues her nervous circular hopping dance until Ms. Biz returns one last time and effortlessly takes the remaining peanut before flying off.

Moral? The first bird shall be last and the last bird shall be first and if you hesitate in fear and intimidation, Ms. Biz will unfailingly get the most peanuts.

Epilogue: I am happy to report that I have become a bit more like Ms. Biz and that Lily McClellan has not been seen in these parts now for some time. Unfortunately, however, as of this writing, Big Bill and the tittering female have not yet realized that they lost all the peanuts they once thought they had so cleverly gathered. Not to worry. There will always be a new election opportunity, but this time Ms. Biz will *foot* the bill.

BUG CHATTER
[a suite of creative non-fiction shorts drafted in the workshop]

EMILY HEEBNER

Pests

She screams at me, this one; then he shouts at her. Crazy, these two.

"A-a-a-a-a," she shrieks, as I fall out of the cupboard, tumbling off the tile counter, cracked and pink, onto the wood floor.

Oo, bagel crumbs, yum.

Off I go, through the crack in the floor board, under the greasy slat, hiding against the thicker section where they never step. Safe. Boy, that screamer, she won't stop...

"You've got to do something! I can't live like this!" she wails.

"There's something wrong with you," he says, in his quiet, calm baritone. "It's just a bug."

"It's not a bug, it's a cockroach! I've never seen such a big cockroach! My big toe's not as big as that damn cockroach! He fell out of the cupboard - I can't have that - I can't live in a place where big toe-size cockroaches leap out of the kitchen cupboard!"

"Okay," he says quietly, "then don't."

She's stopped screaming now. Maybe I can take my nap.

JEAN WAGGONER

Bzzzt!

[deer fly stream-of-consciousness]

Bzzt! This animal doesn't smell too good. It's got that dead metal giant moving thing odor about it. You know, oily. Still, there's no other meat on the hoof around today -- none since these two-legged things started making so much noise all over the place. There aren't even any of those yummy four-legged leaping things with the mean hooves at the stream for a drink. Bzzt! I guess I need to aim for a spot of flesh that doesn't stink too much.

Bzzzz...zz...bzzzz....bzzzz – yikes! It's flapping its dangling non-legs at me! Bzzt! I need to get on one of those parts. Ah, yes...here. Bzzt! Or maybe here – a little more toward the blood's coursing....here! Bzzz.....zzzz....It's a bit wet, less smelly. Now! Here!   C H O M P!

DAVID CALVIN GOGERTY

Musings by a Pholcus Phalangiodes

Phylum: Arthropeda
Class: Arachnida
Order: Araneomorphae
Family: Pholcidae
Genus: Pholcus

Commonly known as Cellar Spider, Skull Spider, or Daddy Longlegs.

Why is that big creature shooting water from a hose at us? All we were doing was hanging out in a group, above one of the front windows of the house. We gather together so that we can communicate better with each other and enjoy each other's company. Some of us do wander off periodically, but when we do, we may be devoured by a hungry member of our own species. When we wander off, it is generally to find insects to eat that have been trapped in the webs that we have spun.

We didn't need to bathe before the big creature turned a hard stream of water on us. All that did was to knock us off of the wall and into the dirt. It will take awhile for us to clean ourselves up and find our separate ways back together, and during all of that time we are at risk of being devoured.

We don't really harm the big creature that shoots water at us twice each week. We create attractive webs attached to his house and the nearby plants. Our webs are engineering marvels, effective at attracting other insects. Maybe if we were to eat the captured insects sooner, rather than cocooning them for later feasting, the webs would be more attractive. But, why should we fit our eating schedules to suit the unknown desires of big creatures?

Maybe the big creatures are afraid of us, but we don't know why. We have noticed that if we land on one of the big creatures, they brush us off as soon as they notice us. Maybe they are afraid that we will bite them. All of us Pholcidae, and the many varieties of our cousins in the Araneomorphae order, are all poisonous. That is how we kill insects and other small prey. Why would we bite the big creatures, except to protect ourselves? We don't have enough venom to give them anything but a minor stinging sensation, which lasts only a few minutes. They don't taste very good; it would be impossible to cocoon them for later feasting; and they are too large to devour in any reasonable time. They are strange creatures that we will never understand.

Dinner Time

Here comes dinner
 right on time,
The light is low.
The fly looks fine.

She'll never see my work of art
 And as such now
My first course is her part.

But now look yonder!
There Comes Dessert.
 That soft moth
 will feel this hurt.

Another night at this corner...
 I think tomorrow
 I'll try the dormer.

Kosmos, Palms

INLANDIA CREATIVE WRITING WORKSHOP - PALM SPRINGS
LED BY MAUREEN ALSOP

CONTRIBUTORS

Cynthia Anderson - Lec Balan - Michael Bennett
Alaina Bixon - Alissa Bixon - Nancy Scott Campbell
Glen Fitch - Noreen Lawlor - Jacqueline Mantz Rodriguez

CYNTHIA ANDERSON

Self-Portrait in a Convex Faucet

Why does my eye
fall where it falls?
The shine of chrome
forms a mirror,
the essence of surprise,
as I lean over the sink
and find myself doubled,
with no more substance
than a passing cloud.
The woman I see there
has a face intensified
by worry and age, yet a torso
that whispers out of time,
miraculously youthful
through a trick of perception.
Outside, the low roar
in the pines tells me
the wind is up—a sound
I know intimately,
like the pounding of blood
in my body, a sound
I could listen to forever,
and would, if given the chance—
but, having only the moment,
I grab my camera, hold it
over my face, and click.

Tomography

Connected to life support
A thin line between life and death
Air supply
Floating in the black void
Above the surface of the moon
Earth's handmaiden
Mining resources to sustain life
Helium-3 to ship back home
Ragged breathing
Connected to hoses
Life support
Blinking monitors
Old man still conscious
Trying to speak
Last words
You hear music far away
Stevie Nicks sings Rhiannon
Blurred vision
Sentinels in white
Hover like birds of prey
M.D. checks phone for news
"President hung in effigy
Wars escalate"
Pictures of angels flash on TV down the hall
Switching channels
Ads for 3D
Future technology on ten sixty-three
Traversing the Event Horizon
Time travel
Assassination
Viet Nam
1969
Moon landing
Tripping on acid

First time
Melon lady
Gushing fruit
Flowing nectar
Naked warrior with red hair
Arousal
Facing demons
Just barely surviving
Escaping Earth's gravity
Crash landing
Breathing through gasmask
Last words
"No angels
No miracles"

Assessment

Lloyd is a corporate entity
   Taking photographs with his Blackberry
I mimicked ignorance
   Blending like a chameleon
I understand the gravity of the situation
   Ill-liquidity in accountant lingo
The night before
   I exposed myself
   Convinced it was the path to redemption
      My naked soul on the auction block
I needed cash
   The return was insubstantial
      I was out on my ass

The wall in my living-room is malleable
Lips appear
   Emerge and hover by my ear
      Whispering

Lloyd is from the future
   Dressed in black
He offers advice about investments
I mention the ill-fated auction
"No worries" he says and takes more pictures
   Assessing the depreciation
I return to my painting
   Started in 1976
Hoping to discover the meaning

At night I watch TV

HWY. 62 to Yucca

He called to tell me he'd been robbed and beaten by three men in Desert Hot Springs. I was amazed, not by the beating but by the phone call. I hardly knew the man. He was simply someone a friend had brought by the house once, several months ago. A few weeks later, his name came up in connection with a girl who almost died while the two of them were together, doing some designer drug. That was it, the full extent of our acquaintance.

I remember saying something vaguely sympathetic about the beating; probably a mistake because he then said he had no money and nowhere to go. Could he stay at the house for a couple of days? That wasn't possible, I told him. He said he understood and then made a second request. Would I give him a ride to his father's house in Yucca Valley? He didn't seem like a person to seek solace from family so perhaps this was more about getting a few bucks and a place to crash.

The one time we met he struck me as unremarkable, cobbled together from contrived elements I'd seen a thousand times before; the long hair, tattoos, the attitude, and honestly, the end product was less interesting than the individual parts. I'd pretty much forgotten him except for briefly hearing his name when the girl's story made the rounds. I hadn't paid much attention then. Now, assuming the story was true, I was suddenly curious to know what actually happened, although I wasn't sure it had anything to do with the decision I currently needed to make. He had asked for a ride. Providing the ride was something I could easily do. The request seemed to come with a sense of urgency and I couldn't think of a good reason to refuse. Perhaps, at that moment, I remembered the joys of spontaneous acts, or was feeling benevolent or simply bored. Whatever the reason, I asked where he was and told him to wait; I'd be there soon.

The night was unusually cold. As I pulled up, I spotted him immediately, a solitary figure waiting outside the Emergency Room entrance, shivering. Walking to the car, his movements were deliberate; a cracked rib was my guess. Now closer, I barely recognized him. One eye was swollen shut and the area around it was purple and black with bruising. His left arm was in a cast and a large patch of hair was gone where a nasty laceration in his scalp had been closed with surgical staples. Although his tattoos were covered and I assumed still intact, now part of

32

his head was shaved and there was no attitude. He looked smaller. "Thanks" he mumbled, turning away to stare out the side window. I pulled onto Indian Canyon and headed north.

"When did it happen?" I asked, after we'd driven a while in silence.

"This morning; these three motherfuckers beat the shit out of me," he said. "One used a fucking metal pipe!"

He went quiet, and for a moment I thought he'd finished, but then he took a deep breath, as if to re-group, and continued.

"They came from behind. I never saw their faces." he said. "Cold motherfuckers, fucking took all my money."

"Did they say anything" I asked?

He shook his head no, still turned away, as he had been, staring out the window the entire time he told the story.

It was an odd story; not that I doubted what he'd told me but something was missing. Perhaps it was as simple as eye contact while he spoke. I found myself waiting and realized I hadn't reacted. Normally I'd have been outraged or sympathetic; felt some strong emotion. Now I felt…what? Removed; I simply felt removed and an ugly little voice, bobbing like a mischievous cork, kept whispering a single word; *unseemly,* again and again.

I drove on, mentally re-visiting my tepid response, trying to understand, but it soon became clear my appetite for self analysis was leading nowhere. What had been so compelling a moment earlier was now simply annoying; useless speculation. I mentioned a couple I thought he might know, looking for distraction in some mindless conversation. Yes, he told me, he really liked the woman and her boyfriend, but felt it wasn't cool that he beat on his old lady.

"That's probably over," I told him. "I've heard she checked herself into rehab and finally had the boyfriend charged with domestic violence."

He seemed surprised, then smiled and gave a small shrug. "Hey man," he said, "they're all bitches."

I said nothing, but began questioning the wisdom of this trip and knew that sinking, in-the-pit-of-my-stomach feeling was fast approaching as I calculated exactly how bad a mistake I'd made. No, I'm not doing that, I decided, at least not yet, and kept driving.

As we turned onto Hwy. 62, I noticed the sky. It was jet-black and filled with stars. The road unfurled before me as if it would take me to the other side of the planet and I remembered a trip I'd taken with a buddy one summer, years ago, when we were seventeen, filled with the intoxication of new discoveries, cruising down deserted inter-states, in the middle of the night, in the middle of nowhere; our futures were as wide open as the roads ahead.

"Mind if I smoke?" I heard him ask, jerking me back to the present.

I said I didn't and cracked the window. He took a deep drag and slowly exhaled.

"Me and my dad's relationship is really fucked," he said, eyes closed, speaking more to himself than to me. "I want us to get along. It'll be hard work but I can do it. I fucking know I can. It'll be fucking amazing!"

Well, I thought, you've got lots of company. Seemed like half the men I knew still had issues around that relationship. As if he'd read my thoughts, he opened his eyes, turned to me and, perhaps to prove his situation was a bit more than 'having issues', said, "The last time I saw my dad, he told me if I ever came back, he'd fucking kill me."

"Christ!" was all I could manage. That amused him.

"He's really not so bad," he laughed. "Come in with me tonight. Fucking meet him!"

His father sounded like some mean drunks I'd known. Dealing with mean drunks; Thanks, not interested. I told him it was late; I'd probably just drop him off and head back. He said nothing, but I caught the look of disappointment flash across his face.

We pulled into Yucca Valley a bit before 10 p.m. It seemed much later. The streets were deserted, covered in an icy slush and piles of dirty snow had formed by the sides of the road. His father's house was remote, off an unpaved road, but eventually we found it. I pulled up next to the front fence and kept the motor running; loving the heater and impatient for the son's door to open.

"Sure you won't come in," he asked again, "just for a minute?"

"Thanks," I said, "I'll pass."

He made no move to go, but simply sat there, for what seemed too long a time, gazing up at the house. "I don't want to go in there alone." he finally said.

Between the cold, the frozen ground and his injuries, getting him up to the house was slow going. We finally reached the door; he rang the bell and we waited, both of us out-of-breath and shivering. It felt like more snow was coming. The door opened and a skinny old man stood there, dressed in a dirty work shirt, pajama bottoms and a pair of slippers, holding a water glass full of what looked like bourbon. He glanced at his son who, by some weird sleight-of-hand, was now behind me. Then, shifting his focus, he studied me.

"Dad, this is my friend who gave me a ride from Palm Springs" the son suddenly announced, in a manic jabber, "You're really going to like him. He's a great guy!"

This flood of explanation rode in on a single breath, only to vanish immediately as the old man walked back into the house, totally ignoring his son. I realize it may not have been a fully conscious act, but I found myself following him, the son still planted behind me. When we reached a large recliner in the living room, the old man stopped to fulfill what I suspect he believed to be his only obligation as a host.

"You want a drink?" he asked, not bothering to turn towards me.

When I declined, he eased himself onto the recliner. Then his drink, held lovingly, seemed to move in slow motion, in an arc through the air until he placed it within arm's reach on a small table. And at the moment it came to rest, I saw, waiting on that small table, like an unexpected punch-line, the gun. I stood frozen, unable to shift my bovine gaze. I felt certain the old man kept me in his sights the entire time he went about retrieving his drink, taking a sip and finally picking up the gun.

"For protection," he said. "Never know who might show up."

I found the closest chair and sat. Well, I thought, here we go! The son started to tell his father about the beating but was cut off. "You probably deserved it," his father snapped; his son's guilt a given. Then, turning to me, he announced "The kid's worthless!" and began listing, in detail, all his son's failures over the last thirty-some-odd years, waiving the gun as a type of punctuation. I looked around, wondering how to be somewhere else. The son insisted he'd changed and, speaking a bit too quickly, began providing examples. Finally, perhaps more supplication than a statement, he said "You'll see, Daddy. You'll see and be proud of me."

A moment later, I heard long intakes of breath as the son began sobbing while his father turned away in disgust. The evening had just become a master class in pain. The father was despicable, yet how many lies, I wondered, how many broken promises, how many of my things stolen to buy drugs would it take for me to become as bitter and vicious as this old man?

The son sat slumped in a chair; quiet, looking forlorn. What was it he'd expected this time from a father who treated him with such contempt, and if the expectation included anything even remotely kind, how, I wondered, does a person maintains that level of hope?

Certainly I'd known other men like the son; guys too old to still be seeking their father's approval; who lied and hated women and made a big point of telling you how much they loved pussy, yet this particular man was an enigma. After what I'd seen, I continued to feel almost nothing; little empathy or compassion for him, only detachment. What was it about him that evoked in me such coldness? I was exhausted. It felt like I'd been there for days. My head hurt. I couldn't think about any of this now.

I gazed around the room. The son was still in the chair but was now reanimated by a second attempt at describing the beating; this time pointing at his various injuries as if they were stigmata, offering irrefutable proof of his goodness and worth. His father sat turned away, oblivious; sipping his drink and not listening, never listening. Another cycle had begun. I stood up and walked over to the son.

"Get up," I said. "You're leaving!"

Travel Advisory

This life is a hospital where each patient is possessed with the desire to change beds; one prefers to suffer in front of the stove, and another believes that he would recover beside the window.

It always seems to me that I should feel well in the place where I am not, and this question of moving is one which I discuss incessantly with my soul.

Charles Baudelaire, excerpted from "Anywhere Out of the World" from *Les Fleurs du Mal,* 1857

Every night around three, public radio adds selections to what I consider the Don't Go Travel Brochure. Listening to long, gritty dispatches on BBC and NPR replaces my own nightmares with nonfiction horror.

Pakistan. What century are you living in?

Calcutta, where plastic sheeting counts as housing for large families without sewer systems or clean drinking water.

The Ganges River has become synonymous for the annual religious pilgrimage which invariably includes a stampede, sinking ferry boat, or collapsing bridge.

Cairo. You can Google amazing images of the pyramids, crisper than any photo you could capture with your phone. Bonus: you don't have to be there.

And speaking of capture, try to avoid the regions – not limited to Central America and Somalia – where the main source of revenue is holding foreigners for ransom.

Siberia

Mongolia

Iraq

Iran

Afghanistan. If only I could go back to not knowing where it is, other than that tiny, inexpensive restaurant in North Beach with the lamb/ pumpkin curry.

Chechnya

Lagos, even though a friend who worked for the State Department said she once had a big house with servants there.

Morocco

Bogotá

Algeria

Anyplace along the Arizona/Mexico border, which *is* Mexico.

Moscow. If you must go, hire an English-speaking driver with designer sunglasses and a bullet-proof Mercedes.

Phuket. See notes regarding pirates.

Madrid. Here the only bad thing is you will be pickpocketed several times in one week, but you may decide the art and tapas made it worthwhile.

Kurdistan

Tajikistan, even if those beautiful necklaces of hammered metal are made there. Find them at World Market instead.

Abidjan

Belarus

Dakar

Avoid destinations that require special inoculations against dengue, yellow fever, plague, or malaria. Do not travel to a location where you must land by helicopter or carry a water purification kit. Add to this list any place where women are not allowed to drive.

Bangladesh

Uzbekistan

Mogadishu

Tunis. If the ship docks in this port, don't leave your cabin. "Let me take you to the Kasbah" still translates, in local parlance, to "Kiss your ass goodbye."

Waziristan. Some instinct warns me that this particular region is the Anti-Christ of travel experiences, a level of hell beyond Dante's imagining. Don't be tempted, even if the hotel promises to upgrade you to a suite (there are no suites in Waziristan).

The steam lockers in the storage facility of my mind are piled high, stuffed like a piroshky with brochures and alluring images of exotic places. Some are gorgeous, some mysterious, others remote or forbidding.

A vast world, brimming with destinations, lies out there.
Stop. Don't think. Don't go.

At dawn I fall asleep and dream of Fiji.

It's Been Real

1/16" and 1/8" Allen wrenches are enclosed, along with wheels and
   knobs. No other tools are required for assembly.

This will just sting a tiny bit.

I see your point.

Babe, call you soon.

Less tar, more flavor.

We can handle this.

Builds healthy bodies 12 ways.

Non-scorch pans.

No, really, that haircut looks good on you.

I'll be back in time, no sweat.

This river has never overflowed.

It's gold-plated, so it won't discolor.

My wife is totally different from you.

One size fits all.

It's just as easy to take care of two dogs as one.

The battery on my phone must have died, or I would have heard you calling.

Most people are proud to have served on a jury.

You're going to make so much money.

Let me see, that was four strokes.

Yeah, we can bring this baby in on time, no problemo.

Fragile – handle with care.

Satisfaction guaranteed.

Satisfaction guaranteed, or your money back.

I only had one glass of wine with dinner, officer.

Driver's license – height.

Driver's license – weight.

In five years, we'll look like geniuses.

Most people are back at work a week after the procedure.

I've never done this with anyone before.

We'll take this to our graves.

Think of these classes as an investment for your future.

Hold on, there's just two minutes left in this game.

I'll always love you.

This baby gets 39 miles per gallon.

In a couple of years, you just refinance to a new low start rate.

Someday we'll look back at this and laugh.

You'll feel a slight pressure.

It's not you; it's me.

I've got your back.

Institutionalization

all the i's
crouched between consonants
a flimsy handle to hold,
i fell from the transit,
from the insti, tuti, zati.

they rode off without me,
i yelled at them all night,
i couldn't stop screaming
at your blank face.

you sat as if you owned the seat,
smiling into the air,
as if everyone could hold on,
as if you had never kicked a dog.

i had no time to stop at the market.
to buy the things you asked for.
i had to catch the transit
to arrive in situ
at the alizarin station.

Heap

There's a shirt on the floor
Where did the damn thing come from.
But that's not all.
Piles of papers and books, cans of wall paint,
a hammer, an earring, a cloisonné egg,
clothes to be repaired.
I can hardly walk through here.
If I don't get rid of it
Someone will have to.

Dig a hole. Throw it in. All of it.
No, not that! It's precious to me.
I paid too much.
I paid to little.

Who can rest with everything nattering
about where it came from, about
what strange process of manufacture,
all the raucous energy against entropy.

Get rid of it! I want to sweep the floor,
to be here, sweeping the floor.
I want to stop piling it up, stop
the manufacture of word commodities,
bedspread backstreet billow blue cowl clink
glabrous fungible frangipani flotsam fox trot.

Mask

As we talked, I saw myself in the mirror.
Seeing myself seeing you
was like looking down an endless road
where trees arch over the center like brows.

What a shock that you could see me.
I thought I was just a voice making comments.
But there it was, the center of my lip run amok,
Well known from private viewings.
I do not take this lightly,
this being so redolent of flesh and feature.
I prefer delivering my aperçus
from the ether.
Men have tried to penetrate me;
it was like trying to tack froth to a wall.
There is something they see,
but It was just a voice wearing shoes.

generations of genes float

through this oval mirror
strong-minded square jaws
foreheads broad as the atlantic they
once crossed
that would be father's side

and there
I can make out some of mother's
her baby fine hair a halo
counterpoint to what she called
the big mouth now in me
an embarrassment of words
I see her long neck ghost
into the mahogany frame of this old
echo more ripe than I

yes the heirloom itself has age-spots
and maybe what it deserves
causing a few to feel awful about
what they've seen over the years
but not me no I feel
amused at its flaws
what the mirror cannot show like
where it's been what it's done
the wonder of me
and how it will all stop

if I have my way

extinction won't be forever
take that ranch chicken
caged and squatting above
her own ammonia and
fed hormones that force
her to lay day after day

can't move there's no air
it's dark and
on a whim or out of boredom
beneath the feathers
she sees inside
the possibility

here within hen milieu
on a twisted double helix
her ancestors perch and brood
ancient dinosaurs lure
temptation ten
thousand suns strong
no choice for the hen

she transforms
becomes the dinosaur
maybe a menacing
carnivorous kind
a raptor who can capture
and coop humans like
chemists the cage maker
agri-people
slaughter men
the consumer and
on and on

all of us
we're fed bone
while the raptor and her kind
prepare to eat a whole
city of us

amazing
I hear one raptor think
Malibu tastes just like chicken

GLEN FITCH

What the Martian Didn't See

He saw a two inch rock amid the sand.
He saw three sections with three lobes across.
He blinked his eye and dropped it with a toss
And poked another with his sucker hand.
I saw a shield-like shell of armored scales,
Saw tentacle-like eyes, a sword-like spine.
I watched it hover, waiting for a sign
To dart and gulp some shrimp who squirms and flails.
He didn't see a creature lost a mile
Above, five hundred million years away
From home, transformed from flesh to lime and clay,
And trapped in layered time in pile on pile.
He saw "as is." But what he couldn't see:
A trilobite is awe and irony.

Flesh

My palm fits bulge to curve. So heavy, firm,
Your freckled skin conceals a softer spot.
Your spicy scent betrays a hint of rot.
Your pentagram protects the magic germ.
I pull you close to view your nether side.
I fear I'll find a flaw or wound or scar.
Below I spy the sun-shy withered star.
Within the past and future both reside.
Once grateful hunters asked the beasts they'd slain
To grant them their forgiveness with a prayer.
Just so I close my eyes. My teeth I bare.
My body, breed and spirit to maintain,
I lick my lips with poison. I prepare
For gritty, crisp and gushious bursts of pear.

Crayon Tin

I miss their greasy feel, their subtle scent.
In my hot fists, they jostled, trading specks.
I prized the ones with gold or sliver flecks.
Some wear my spit. I made that milk tooth dent.
There's almond, chestnut, eggplant, copper, or
Canary, coral, ruby, sapphire, jade
Or olive, orange, lime or onyx shade
Or orchid, rose. Each hue's a metaphor.
I learned which ones to use on pad or page
For waxy waves, skies soapy, chalky rocks.
Some broken in their sleeves, by use they age.
For years most stood attention in their box,
A rainbow of potential all infused.
Like me they wait unrealized, unused.

A loaf of white bread

flour flecks fly
dance off the miller's fingers
white as Whitsunday vestments
pale as moths' mouths
or mouths of moths
which is the month of the
White Witch Moth
say that three times
where to put the apostrophes
apostles of days
we dream nocturnal emissions
commissions for Lilith (succubus)
come our wild mother feed
the unstoppable clatter
of Hummingbirds' tongues
Snow Leopards leap
through light lengths
between the rods and cones
of eclectic impulses
color vast canvases
bare as sodomized dawn
rare sides of beef
bloodshot eyes
blasphemed mana
hoc est corpus meum

The Three Little Girls

A Sea of Brassy Day

There was a chlorinated sea once upon a time. A turquoise pool infused with slants of golden sunlight. The strokes of a little girl's browned flesh flapped against the water, lap after lap; a foamy background to the day. Her curly head moved to the left to breathe, to the right to breathe, and to the left again, like some nursery rhyme yet unwritten. Another little girl almost a mirror replica of the first one except a little chubbier, lay buried in bubbles, battling in the Jacuzzi against dragons of steam. The little girl's toes sworded through the water as she held onto the edge of the pool floating on her back. The third little girl, the youngest, floated across that same water making animals from clouds in a bubble above her head. Her long dark hair fanned out, an ode to Ophelia in her watery grave.

Their father, dear father, sizzled thick steaks on the grill, a cigarette in one hand a spatula in the other, smoke filling the air. The florescent yellow potato salad and rolls sat quietly on the scarred picnic table, paper plates and the plastic tub of margarine keeping them company. The three little girls, for some reason, at the same moment, all took a deep breath and inhaled Kool menthol cigarettes mixed with charred flesh, a deeply satisfying dysfunctional potion.

Just then their mother, dear mother, suddenly appeared in a Chinese red smock soiled with bits of greasy foo young and shrimp. Her eyes tabulated magically, with one look, the empty Budweiser cans. The mother frowned, then her eyes moved to the three little girls. Ordering them out of their sea of fun; to lie one after the other on blue and white faded striped bath towels; lying, drying baking. Three little girls with waiting tummies growling for rib eyes steaks and mustardy onion infested potato salad that even now they taste and savor.

Once upon a time, this azul rectangular sea would hold the middle girl, the chubby twin, during the day and soothe her at night. Just knowing it lay outside her window gave the little girl; all the three little girls most likely, courage to face the dawning night. This simple body of water gave the girls the strength to survive the nights of shadows making puppet monsters on the ceiling and closet door, nights reeking of rising words in a Holly Hobby oven of hate.

The three little girls never knew when their slumber would be transformed into dense forests of fear, when their father, dear father, would wander away from home into bars. Then, only then, would those three little girls be thrown into a nightmare of hiding on the roof or running underneath tears of stars. Sometimes, more than once, they would flee to the park, but a block away... Yet this land could not be the same as the one they lived in during the day; it could not be. They were somewhere else, a Nightmare Never Neverland.

The girls would stay in the pool in the glittering day as long as they could. Under the covers in the darkening night, they would try to do the same; trying to remember the pool was out there. Trying to remember, that tomorrow no matter what happened, they would all be there in the land of turquoise sea, in the sun, alive and well.

Dawning Night

John Wayne's last film *The Shootist* was on the television. The three little girls played Monopoly in the living room as their dear father watched television, smoking cigarette after cigarette as "The Duke" played a dying man with cancer. If the three little girls could time travel, they would see their father ironically playing that same story out in thirty years, wheezing out his last breath, the dark magician of death waving the wand of pancreatic cancer to seal their father's fate, two months after diagnosis. Maybe, if the wife had access to this crystal ball, she would have been kinder, more loving and less sharp with words to her dear husband. Maybe if the mother would have gazed back into that crystal ball, she might have seen the damage she would cause the three little girls with her fits of chaotic rage.

Maybe is a hideous word, ugly in its hope. There were no maybes as the night dawned dark and heavy with tension curtaining the house with every throw of the dice. The twins fought over a move in the game. The older twin cheated, the younger twin threw the board. The youngest sat there calmly as the two bickered, made up, and the game resumed. It was Saturday night and cleaning time for their dear mother. She washed clothes, picked up the mess left by cyclones of childhood, and cussed the entire time. The three little girls paid it no mind; they knew danger, but it had not yet appeared. The father's show ended. Now it was night. Darkness settled over the land as did the flight in the father's soul.

"I'll be right back, girls," the father slurred, "I need cigarettes and more Budweiser. I'll bring you each back a present. I shall get you a Payday, you a Big Hunk and you a Twix." He patted each girl's head as he walked slowly out the door.

"Daddy hurry home, ok?," said the youngest. The father walked out into the night. The night filled with plenty of maybes. *Maybe I'll just stop for one drink at The Palomino, one game of pool.* The mother heard the blue Ford pick-up truck's engine as she moved the clothes into the dryer. She walked into the house with a plastic basket filled with clothes.

"Stop playing that game. Help me fold these clothes," the mom ordered. The girls silently began folding the clothes, their sibling bickering done. They were one now. A climate of fear pervaded the house.

"Where did your dad go?" the mother asked. She was already different, the metamorphosis had begun.

"He went to go get beer and cigarettes," the eldest answered, "and he will be right back, he said so." There was no answer from the mom. The minutes ticked by, each longer than the last. Five minutes turned into ten minutes, ten minutes to eleven, to twelve, to thirty. The Monopoly game was put away, as were the clothes. The three girls took their baths. Still the father did not reappear. Thirty minutes became an hour. The hand of the clock shoved and pushed the mom's rage higher; now cuss words were dangerous blows. They fled from them, from the TV, into the middle twin's room as it was the furthest away from their once dear mother who changed, with warning even, into the darkest of witches. One whose wild curly hair and words made them cringe. They sat in the middle girl's room and looked at the pool, reflecting on the day.

"We had so much fun today. We should go to sleep," the eldest girl said. The words made sense logically but words of logic did not rule this dark land.

"I want to look at the pool," said the youngest, "I don't want to go to sleep. We might have to get up." They sat on the bed quietly, the door closed against the spells of rage and the curses against them and their dear father…Then, the roar of the witch's car. How long did they have? How many minutes would it take the witch to drive from their home to the bar and back? What if he was at a different bar? How long to the next bar? Experts they were at grabbing blankets, pillows and jackets. Out into the night they went, hoping no one would see their shame. What fairytale law had they broken to take away their kingdom and transport them to this one? Their footsteps were almost silent. They knew the way to the park. They knew their way back it was only over the corner to the right. The park was their night fortress. The park was their mother now that the witch had taken over their dear mother's form.

They made it in five minutes, and lay inside the stinky pee king of cheese. They lay together, feet in sneakers, with their pajama bottoms poking out of their jackets. The twins had Wonder Woman pajamas on. They loved The Justice League. The youngest girl's Snow White long nightgown shone in the moonlight. A long time they slept, awakened by the calls of the witch out the car screaming for them.

"Not yet, he's not home yet. I can tell by the sound of her voice," whispered the youngest. The three little girls fell back into a non-deep sleep for what seemed like days, the longest of nights. The middle girl, the chubby twin, dreamt of the sea outside her window. In her dream, she and her sisters swam in slants of golden sunlight surrounded by the azul waves created by the strokes of their arms in unison stroke after stroke.

The Darkest Night Fled Suddenly As Did The Witch.

"Girls, come home. Girls, come home. Girls, come home," called a voice. The dear mother returned with the retrieval of the drunken father found finally in the bar of *The Palomino*

"Come get him. He was fast asleep on the toilet, good thing I clean the restrooms before locking up." The owner had called the house at 2 am just when the witch was throwing out all of the father's clothes on the front lawn.

"Girls, come home. Girls, come home…" No more words best left to the devil. The three little girls were no longer hated. They were loved and even though it was night, they could once again feel the sun's rays upon them. They came willingly into the car. They walked like puppets, strings pulled by the mother's fingers, into the house where on the table lay a Payday, a Big Hunk and a Twix.

SLOUCHING TOWARD MT. RUBIDOUX MANOR

INLANDIA CREATIVE WRITING WORKSHOP - RIVERSIDE
LED BY RUTH NOLAN

CONTRIBUTORS

Hong-My Basrai - Karen Bradford - Nikia Chaney
Mike Cluff - Deenaz P. Coachbuilder - Avika Dhillon
Harki Dhillon - Heather Dubois - Cyrus Emerson
Amy Floyd - Carissa Garcia - Michelle Gonzalez
Joan Koerper - Marc Lombardo - Jan Lucas
Juanita Mantz - Lorraine Naggi Peter Naggi
Kamelyta Noor - Mike Sleboda - Steve Vaughn
Mae Wagner - Jean Waggoner - J. Ladd Zorn

Watching Papi

How on earth did he end up being dragged here and left in this large house smelling faintly of steamed rice and fish sauce? Who was this person, his *papi*–old, strange…a stranger?

He was taught to call this man *papi* from the time he learned of his grandpa's presence by the old man's approaching knees. Then his recognition included the man's broad face–shrouded eyes, Oriental features, flared nostrils–his careful, measured voice, his shuffling gait carrying a huge pot belly on a slightly stooped frame. Yet what he had learned about the man never deepened into affection. His mind had developed the folds of knowledge, but his heart was not affected by the familiar sight of his grandpa although he had been around often.

At each visit, in the presence of this old relative he called *papi*, the little Josh used to pull on his mother's pant leg, demanding to be picked up; the man's strange face with a thick, flattened nose scared him.

The years had worked magic on the boy, transforming him into a tall young man with the shadow of a mustache on the upper-lip. But seventeen additional winters were detrimental to the bent old man, eating away his speech to bare necessity and deadening his walk. The stranger had become harder to relate to with his hesitant movements, his lapses of memory, his sealed-away world. As the boy soared into the world of possibilities, the grandpa receded back into a shell. The gap between them was larger than one between generations, deeper than one that divided different cultures, or one that separated the sexes; the unfillable schism between two souls that never loved one another.

In those seventeen years, the erratic exposures to his grandpa did not bring the boy closer to him. The knowledge of this old relative had stopped at the surface, at the face like a full moon, at the short stature that seemed to shrink farther each year, at the pot belly. Josh never knew him enough to participate in a conversation with him. The few attempts coerced by his mom had been awkward and artificial for both men, old and young.

At every visit, his grandpa addressed the boy diplomatically with his perfect English, in well-measured words that did not go beyond the casual greetings and simple questions. "You've grown tall" was the latest repeated remarks. To his daughter, the man spoke in their shared chopping, monosyllabic language whose sound was familiar to Josh but incomprehensible, like the chirping of a bird.

The sight of this imposing Asian man with his halting steps still caused the boy, now half-man, to recede back into his room for fear of another encounter. Except for the stiff and courteous greetings each time they met, except for the discreet nod to acknowledge each other's presence, the relationship his mom thought would be naturally enhanced by time had never taken roots, and her attempts to hasten its growth had forever stunted it. The burden of the blood tie was to Josh akin to an embellished cravat that he wore on solemn occasions. With Grandpa, he could not be himself. He could only force the casual talks, not the affection.

He did not plan to be here to keep watch on his grandpa. The boy gave the sleeping man a suspicious look: he was reclining on the living room's sofa, eyes closed—more like a bloated corpse, but with his mouth still working the air, blowing in and out.

"Something was not right with him," had reported Aunt Hue-Mei earlier over the speaker of his mom's cell phone.

At first, Aunt Hue-Mei had thought that it was one of those age-related temporal dizzy spells. But when the old man did not improve, she suspected something worse.

"It could be a mild heart attack."

Prompted by the urgency of her sister's voice, Josh's mom had made a detour and instead of driving him home directly after school, had brought him to Aunt Hue-Mei's home, where *papi* had lived for the last ten years after he had married another wife.

The step-grandma lived separately from the man in a senior home. She came down to this side of town by bus to visit him five days a week, and every weekend she brought him back with her. Josh thought about the strange life of his grandpa that had affected the whole large family for a while now, pitting one group of aunties against another who supported their father's choice, and now, that erratic decision of the old man was messing up the boy's schedule. He was supposed to be at his computer at the most important competition against the best of the best Star-Craft team. Freakin' annoying!

At arrival, they had found his grandpa in this exact position, with only a groan as response when they greeted him. Aunt Hue-Mei handed her sister the portable phone to finish the conversation with their brother and left for the daycare center to pick up her toddler daughter.

Josh only heard her say, "I don't think it necessary to call 911," before she interrupted the conversation and in turn, dialed his dad to relate her recent ordeal. She repeated to her bedfellow all the phone conversations with the various members of her large family and asked whether she should call for emergency assistance for something as benign as a dizzy spell. While this conversation was going on, she said hurriedly, "I'll call back. Someone is trying to get through. Bye, bye now," then switched to, "Hallo, Sister Hue-Ma. Yeah, I'm here with him. What?"

The strident cackling from the other end drifted into Josh's ears. He shifted on the sofa, rolled his eyes and blurted an irritated, "Jesus! Mom, I have homework to do."

His mother lent a deaf ear to his behavior. She was now punching the dial button on her BlackBerry, "Honey, Hue-Ma also said I'd better call 911. She said he has less than three hours to completely recover if it is a stroke."

Whatever his dad told her, Josh did not know. But he could guess that she did not heed his wisdom, for she was now punching on her cell again, calling yet another person, probably another relative with better judgment. She usually concurred with the one that spoke the exact lines of her thinking.

"Hue-Mai, thank God you're available. Dad's not well." Of course, Josh thought, sarcastically, she had to hear the words from Aunt Hue-Mai, the medical doctor "with her own private office at Hoag Memorial," the health-god of the family.

After a lengthy repetition of the morning episode and explanation of what she thought could have happened, Josh's mom breathed out, seemingly relieved, "You're right. Cannot be a stroke. Give him a lot of fluid? All right! Bye, bye, I'll do it now."

She eyed Josh now with a harried look, "Josh, give grandpa something to drink. Whatever he likes, Coke, water, juice. As long as he does not dehydrate, he'll get over it."

Josh did not have time to retort or complain, since the home phone rang shrilly and his mom ran to it as the answering machine started: "You've reached the Jou's residence—" she snatched the receiver off the hook and blasted it with, "Hallo, hallo...."

Josh searched the kitchen cupboard for a cup. He spied one tall glass amidst a row of crystal drinking glasses and reached for one. He brought it to the refrigerator and pressed the water dispenser button with the edge of the round lip, and while waiting for the cup to fill, he kept an eye on his grandpa's shape and listened in to the ongoing conversation between his mother and his dad as it was coming to an end with "instead of languishing at the ER for hours."

Then as soon as she replaced the portable back on its stand (another practice she insisted he should develop) so the phone could recharge and never be misplaced. She announced to him, "I have to go get his pills. You stay until I get back."

Josh was flabbergasted, "Come on, Mom. Didn't you hear me? I got tons of homework to do."

She rushed toward the door as if she did not hear, but she heard, for she reprimanded him with her calmest and saddest voice, "I can't believe you, Josh! Grandpa is sick, your own grandpa, and you're moaning about homework."

Then she switched tone, returning to her own self, her voice firm and commanding, "Grandpa could be seriously ill. Or it could possibly be just food poisoning. We don't know yet. You stay with him until I return with his medication. Don't let him walk anywhere unassisted. Keep an eye on him. You hear?"

Josh knew his mother's weak points. It's no use telling her he had the English project due, or whatever else, but he could make her worry about unexpected events, calling on her imaginative ghosts.

He added quickly before she reached the door's round knob, "Mom, I wouldn't know what to do in case he needs to go."

"In case Grandpa needs to use the bathroom?" Her voice made him recoil with shame inside. He reluctantly nodded, but his irritation again mounted and wiped away the better side of him. He stepped up to her as if to strike her, the filled cup still in his hand, "Why are you doing this to me, Mom? He's perfectly fine. He doesn't need me here. Just so silly."

"I can't believe you, Josh. He's not well, something's wrong with him, and you sit there to complain. How can you be like that, Josh, it's your *papi*, for heaven's sake."

"It's not my fault I don't know him. You can't force me."

"I'm not forcing. You know that, Josh. I can't be here with him. And he can't be left alone. Ahh! Why am I wasting my time arguing with you. I'm leaving. Be back in an hour. Call me on my cell if anything happens."

What could happen? He eyed the old man's pale face suspiciously. *God*....Looking at his *papi* in that position–semi-sitting, semi-reclining on the living room's sofa–blowing like a goldfish with his mind absent, present but not actually there, infuriated the boy further. His Mom must have planned this to put him in this awkward position–to be one-on-one with his grandpa, alone with him to face God knew what. Death? Jesus!

For a moment Josh panicked. His grandpa's right foot jerked slightly, as if he was trying to kick the boy away but did not aim well. Josh wanted to help the man's feet up onto the sofa, so that he could lie down on his back and straighten his body out in a more comfortable position. But he was afraid he would cause some further damage to the old man.

He called softly, pressing the cold glass to the man's lips, "*Papi*. Drink. It's good for you." The eyes' lids moved slightly. Josh tilted the glass and watched the liquid wet the swollen lips unhinged, sucking like a baby.

This done, he got up and paced around, looking for a computer in the vicinity. There was an iMac on the kitchen counter, by the phone system. He would have to leave *Papi* out of sight to use that machine. *What if he falls? Or stops breathing?* He was shaken when his cell phone rattled in his pant pocket. *Jesus! What now?*

"Hello, Mom?"

"Everything alright, Josh? How's *Papi*?"

"Fine. When are you gonna be back?"

"I'm done. I have his prescription. Be there in a few minutes."

"Hurry, Mom. *Papi*'s stirring."

Josh flipped his Motorolla shut. He turned around to check on his grandpa and faced the old man's gaze, grayish and worn, but alive, fully awake. He froze at this sight. Sheepishly, the boy opened his mouth to let out a "*Papi*?"

The old man tried to rouse himself into an upright sitting position, pushing on his seat and struggling with his dangling legs.

"You want help?" Josh came forward toward the helpless elder but did not dare to impose.

His grandpa nodded silently. The boy came closer, hesitantly, then decided all-of-a-sudden to overcome his awkwardness. He leaned close to the old man, placed his lean right arm behind the broad back and heaved, pushing the man up straight.

Fully sitting, with both his feet planted on the floor, his *papi* took a long exhale and said brightly, "I feel much better. Okay now. How are you, Josh? Okay?"

How Riverside Lost Its River

When newcomers arrive in this city in a dry river valley in Southern California, they usually remark, "*Riverside?!* Where's the river?" Well...

Once upon a time, long, long ago, people believed there were spirit forms in everything around them: the stars and planets, the air, the earth with its plants and stones and, most importantly, the life-giving water in all its forms.

Just like everyone else, the people who lived around what is now known as Riverside considered these elements as natural parts of their lives and thought of them as part of their families. Like other family members, the elements had their moods, too, and every so often the moods of the elements would change from their friendly forms, losing their patience or becoming angry: the earth trembled and shook violently; the wind blew with such unrelenting force that a person could hardly walk upright; the sun turned from benevolent to blistering and merciless.

Water, however, realized that he alone gave first life to everything in the valley, from cosseting the tiniest seed with gentle spring rains to creating meandering curves in his river bed to soak into Mother Earth and enrich her fields and trees.

Life was so very pleasant in this valley that people were happy and content, except for one young woman. Water learned to recognize this woman when she quietly slipped between the willows to the river's edge so that she could sit alone. Woman often came to his deep, quiet pools to refresh herself, admiring the birds and animals and watching the fish who lived there. When she was dusty, she removed her garments to wash away the dirt or cleanse her very beautiful long hair. When she was tired, she knew where hot springs formed into pleasurably warm pools. Water was so very pleased to be the one to comfort her, seeking around Woman's curves, lingering to soften her lovely, creamy skin. His warm waters swirled around her, gently dissolving her concerns, embracing her secret places; and so he came to know her, to soothe her body and relieve her soul of its unknown sorrows and loneliness.

One evening was different, however, when Woman ran under the canopy of trees to the river and knelt amongst the soft grass in the moonlight, her tears falling into Water's deep pool. Water was very surprised because they were salty, as he did not recognize tears. He whispered to her in great alarm: "Sweetest Woman, what has caused this salty water from your eyes? It cannot be anything I have done to you, is it?"

Woman cried out in fear: "Who is speaking? Where are you? Reveal yourself at once or I will run away before you can harm me!"

Water whispered more softly so that she would be calmed: "It is I, Water, the river spirit, who soothes your thirst when you work and who surrounds you when you bathe in my embrace ... Tell me, what makes you weep?"

"Oh, Water," she sobbed in a small voice. "No man will take me to wed! No one loves me! I am not nearly so lovely to behold as my sisters, and no one will marry me." She looked up at the moon and continued to weep.

Water was perplexed because he did not know the ways of humans. If only she would slip into his hot springs so that he could comfort her! So instead, he whispered again: "I have always thought you are lovely. You are kind to animals; you gaze upon fish instead of capturing them; and you sit quietly at my edge. Give me the night to shift from a river spirit into the form of a man, and I will marry you at once."

Woman was so happy that she cried a little more and then leapt up: "Yes, oh please yes! I will return at dawn, and we shall be married!" She ran away to tell her sisters.

Water was now even more perplexed: How should he look? What should he wear? He was not so familiar with human men because their women fetched their water and carried it to the men; a man did not linger at Water's edge, gazing at his own reflection as did Woman, so Water had never studied a man's face. Just then, Water noticed the reflection of the Man in the Moon shining his own countenance upon the river's surface. "Aha!" Water thought, "there is my answer for a manly face." Water shifted his shape into that of a man, complete and ready to wait for his bride.

At dawn, Woman and her sisters chattered as they approached the river, and she called out: "Husband, my husband! We are here; where are you?"

Water was excited and most pleased to step into the clearing to take her hand, but when Woman saw him, she cried, "What! What are you? You look like the man in the moon with only half a face, a crater for an eye and pits all over your skin! I cannot marry you! I would rather die an old hag than look everyday upon the likes of you!" Woman and her sisters began to laugh ... and laugh and laugh and laugh.

It had never occurred to Water to judge Woman by her own appearance but instead by her happiness when his waters served her needs. Woman and her sisters continued to laugh, saying how stupid Water was to think that the Man in the Moon was handsome. Now Water saw Woman for her true and ugly self as she revealed her unkind heart, the real reason that no one would take her as wife.

Water's own soul, the source of his life-giving powers, began to crumble, and he felt his first human emotions: shame and wanting to die for being ridiculed by the woman he loved, when he had only wished to please her.

Earth felt Water's agony as he trembled in front of scornful Woman and her laughing sisters, so Earth did the only thing she knew could rescue him: She shook her ground so violently that Water disintegrated and returned to his river form, emptying into Earth's many cracks and fissures that now opened, allowing him to disappear through the sand.

To this very day, Water continues his flow --- underground --- in our valley.

And that is how Riverside lost its river.

Streetwalker: because

It is hot
inside the body
and that is
my world, a
glass jar, a cringe
red spear of spectacle. I
pour cups of white
walls down their
shirts, hoping that
one day I could anchor
your bones
to the gospel
sing it is inside being
your being
and witty, and justifying
the way of the fix
into place, the way
the high heels
scream on the concrete, the fisted
dollars, the false doll
hope, the means it
is to an end. I am
a cell of coal
or else a boil wired
of what should
be hope under
my hands it is just
because inside
the body it is hot, and the cloth
caul on my head winding
tight and I am
meaning to see
you feeling need in
me and the body California

proud, I nipped that
anointed cracker, that salt
fix, appreciation
for the mouth, the body,
waiting, walking
here, I fear only the fat
look, the shaky cream
the truck horn curtain call
Inside is hot and
it is just
because tonight I'm a little
bit tired
I draw knees
up to teeth to
night, I need force
grin. Inside the body, hot
and I made
enough and it
is the heat, the way
I'm not buying
it, and the dissonance
in my skin

Streetwalker: the beginning

Something like a small drop of hunger, something hulking, magnanimous in the braid of the room, something scratching.

It is two minutes of sweetness, it is the seed of the body, it is dripping hair and the taste of the topsides of the fist.

Something that burns kisses in my hand, something singing, with no sleeves or simple wants, a cardboard box ripping.

Something that means, and leaves the children crying. Something forbidden and full of soon.

If we could walk from it, serene cottony meat, we would.

Mama

If you try
to live in that
kind of femininity,
holy,
drunken,
small, a wild bird
happy to shake
hips in the thump
of owner
ship, you should learn
silence like bread
a wonder bottled
in little brass feet, a sweep
squeak of powder
a burp
cloth poised on the pin,

if you want to
sit in it
believe in
it in your
need to bind and birth

you should cross those
legs over your plump belly
speak with soda
on your shoulders as if
you are burping
a new costume as
if the dance
sisters of your youth were
raising puppies and cut
leaf leagues that
required paper doll
heads, the kind lathered
up with oil
white stains

if you decided
with fecklessness to
become smug, superior in
deliciousness another damned
face dripping you'll have
to focus
swallow the cough pluck
out the uncertainty
breath, taste
and push
with attitude

CLUFF

San Bernardino Old Fire November 2003

I.

After "Arsenic And Old Lace"
we did not hold the usual
curtain call
praise was not the utmost acme
to us that night.
The audience did not mind,
they were nowhere to be found
with the same identical dread
in their eyes as well.

Steve, Patrice, Ed,
Julie and I
left in costume
to beat the heat
even though
Halloween was less
than a week ago.

The hills were red
for the wrong reasons
plants and homes dissolving
into grainy greyness.

Beth's place
was spared
all except for smoke
and nightmares.

The rest of us
watched the mountains
and saw only red
of both sorts.

II.

Sarajevo after bombing
the smoke an acrid punch
made more heavy
in the near Halloween air:

San Bernardino
above 39th and Foothill
over to Sterling
a gritty war movie
in living black and white
except for
a yellow stove
halfway up Camellia Drive
the pink plastic ball
staring down
the street
non-blinking
at the gawking souls
in smoke and ash free cars
voyuers against their wills
glad they had won
this game
of hopscotch fire
from Mt. Baldy to
a mile and half
from my homespot
in Highland.

Tamara Larkin: Fontana, California
November 2002

Dancing on Arrow Highway
no real direction to go
the street is smooth
for a change
the white lines
visited now
with be reclaimed later
after Vivian and Blanche and Stella
have left me
alone
truly solo
and utterly

abandoned

alone.

Norco Poem # 12

Coming south on Interstate 15
to the left
on the bluff
about forty or so feet
above the laconic,
most days,
Santa Ana River,
a horse's head
made of white rocks
nicely sized,
show its right side
to the mesmerized-
by- many- miles
motorist.

And in the sunlight of 8:17 a.m.,
the horse's eye
its general outline
even the letters "c" and "o"
of Norco written next to it
disappear into the green bank.

And it is now is
2222 years into the future
more or less.

Gourmet Latte Game-
Third Street Riverside, April 2009

Agnes always became Grace
and Henrietta dons the mantle of Helena
Homer morphs into Chip
in this elitist cafe, coffee shop around.

So Clarence is now Cleitus or Colin
depending upon the phase of the moon
be it April, August, October, June or
February and March and November/May.

While Katie decides to rename, cadge herself
Dominique Alexandra,
it sounds foreign and exotic
but she stills lisps just the same.

Now Bertha adapts Brittany as her moniker
but not the shaved head,
aliases are rebellious enough for her
at least at seventeen.

Simultaneously, Morton would use Tyson
excepting that he is a coward
and cannibalism, ear biting
is not his Morty/ Mac/Malcolm's forte.

Clara is at this moment Carla
since it is easier to spell,
Bill transforms into Will
to have more control over His choices of caffeine.

Curtis always alternates
between iced and hot, Ian and Hank, venti and grande, Vic and Gordon,
whipped or no cream
on his way to becoming Les, than who he really is and was before.

Flowing Between Boundaries So Easily- Highland
4:56 a.m. Wednesdays

The freeway traffic
is sporadic and happy
for once
and the possum in the back
is safe from the laughter of crows
the beta fish is angry
it is alone.

My feet curl with joyness
when the coffee maker clicks on,
the strong scent
drags me out of
my nightmare
of never-ending papers to grade
poems to revise
weeds to be pulled...

into
the reality
that all these dreads and drudgeries
are still there
but in the daytime
can I put them off?

Just like I do
in my nocturnal reflections
on the real world.

Grief on a Spring Day

She has now become larger than the earth.
The leaves have borrowed something of her grace,
the winds bear her hidden pain
and have mingled it with the stars.

Knowing she would soon die, I saw her one day
while she conversed with friends
following her children with her eyes,
grieving that she would not know them grown.
Having become stronger than her simple
motherhood and wifeliness might show,
she comforted me at my leaving, when I cried,
bidding her a silent goodbye.

She left us on a spring day.
Now newly weaned birds mistakenly sing
the whole night through.
This is the season of planting and planning
of sunned warmth and whisperings in warm darkness.
It is too difficult. I cannot conceive that
flowers continue to bloom,
and days follow in unbroken progression.
The sun has diminished none of its glory with her death.

The wind that could not share its strength,
the earth that would not let her dream,
the night that should have ceased before she died,
now gently moves each molecule that was herself
into eternal life.

A Time for Eucalyptus
(Dedicated to my son Shahrukh)

It is my birthday today.
"Just a small gift, Mother."
I unwrap a silver-green package.
Lotions to pamper me await my touch.
I lift the lid, the perfume of eucalyptus
rises from the mist of childhood.

With head mildly throbbing,
strained breath, watery eyes,
a fitful child's limbs move restlessly,
waiting for relief. The clock's pendulum slowly
drags before each click. The hushed house waits.

Suddenly, the front door sweeps open.
The house quivers and awakens.
A sari clad figure enters my room.
Mother kisses me. Vibrations of love and energy
encircle me. Stooping, she applies two small drops
of eucalyptus oil upon my pillow.
Breathing deeply, my eyes turn heavy
in contentment.

Now, naked pink trunked eucalyptus trees
hidden among showers of pale leaves
line the banks of Victoria Avenue and
neighborhood lanes.
I shiver in remembrance when
their soothing perfume surrounds me
at the break of rain after a hot dry spell.

She carries this legacy of eucalyptus from
half a world away, my mother,
across the generations,
      in the mists of memory,
to my son.

Cymbidium Orchid Speaks

Young voices bounced against my light
yellow-green leaves and stems.
The warmth of the kitchen seeped into
the rich acidic earth around my roots.
I glowed in the radius of your care,
as you watered me faithfully,
every week sprinkling nutrients through
the many colored rocks that sparkled
around my stem.
The gentle slant of the morning sun
awoke each of my cleansing white petals.
The centers of my blooms were pink
turning almost velveteen red when
the night lights flicked on.

And so I bloomed for months,
knowing, unconcerned, that the time
for wilting, drying and fading
was drawing close.

You threw me out
into the cold wintry world when my petals fell.
Had you but kept me,
I, Cymbidium Orchid,
would have bloomed for you again.

Liberation

She came home that evening
and found no street. They'd
rolled it up and carted it off
in a huge truck, her neighbor said.
She asked permission from friends
on the other side, and walked through
a slit in the fence to reach
her front door. It would do, she thought.

The next day a family moved
into the downstairs, parents
with two children. They were
quiet and well behaved, and even
allowed her to use her kitchen.

Well, it's roomy upstairs, just me,
she thought as she sat on the rim
of her tub in the tiny bathroom.
They knocked on her door and entered.
Ever so politely, they asked her for
her beautiful almond colored skin,
and her curly brown hair.
Carefully, they peeled it off, her skin,
her hair, those tinted fingernails
she was so proud of.

She dissolved, until only her spirit remained.
It gently fluttered into the night
and slid through the folds of the velvet sky.

Two Women

Look at how she hogs the pavement,
forcing me to dodge pot-holes, my soft
silk shalwar drenched with the muddy water
and the refuse of the street.

I see her every morning in her faded choli
and worn sari, surrounded by grimy, energetic urchins,
emptying the left-overs collected nightly
from neighborhood garbage bins
sorting and separating, packaging and bagging them
in brittle plastic containers.

I stop and glare.
Clear-eyed, uncompromising,
she points to the road as if to say,
this bit of pavement is mine for the day.

I comply.

The Canal

The twilight rays
strike the sands of time;
All the while brightly colored flowers
shut their blooms,
and are thus trapped amongst one another.
The false conveyance of the twilight rays,
the dark water of life
runs down a
man made channel
between the gleaming gemlike sands
reflecting the golden light
of the dying sun.
Yet, the underlying darkness cannot be ignored
as the dark clouds descend,
like a sheet of black velvet
obscuring the brilliant stars
for all time.

The Folded Pages of the Past

I fly back
on the wings of memories
to the night
with the hunters' moon
and my youth.
The cold wooden stock of the gun
and its cold metal barrel
rest comfortably in
my gloved hands.
Mist from my breath
mingles with the mist from the river.
I hear the rustling
of the tall sugarcane,
a menacing contrast
to the silent, subservient
wheat field.
The bundled silhouettes
of family and friends
huddled against the cold,
many now lost
in the folded pages of the past.
A bitterly cold night
brings back
a warm fuzzy feeling.
Young as I was then
I felt what it might feel
to be a man.

When Blood Turns to Water

You fly high on a tapestry of lies
deception in every weave,
camouflaged by soaring images
of hope and purity.
You strip the feeble of their fortunes,
a blight on the end of their days.
You pillage and rape and plunder
the dreams of generations
with a cold and indifferent smile,
the loot feeding your debauched life.
Sometimes you come as a stranger,
evil incarnate,
sometime your blood is the same
as you take them to the slaughter.
It is more than evil
when blood
turns to water.

"The Arrest"

The expanse of maroon roofs,
congealed
in the heat and the glare of the afternoon sun,
slowly emerge as distinct homes
bathed in the light of the evening sun.
The cool clear air
now breaks the lethargy.
People and dogs appear
ambulating aimlessly
in between enthusiastic sprinklers
that proudly exhibit golden drops
of dancing water,
color added by the bright blue and red lights
of a police cruiser,
showing an arrest in progress.
Red back pack on the thin shoulders
of a young black boy
sitting on his haunches
looking at
the tight brown uniform
on the strong, white man
with the big, black gun.

The Green Dress

The bright green dress
defeated by the gentle slope
of the shoulders.
The bright lipstick
hiding poorly
life's worry lines.
The severe black hat
drowning the optimism
that could have been.
If only your children
had not left,
if only they would
hold your hand and smile
and walk in the sunshine
with you,
if only your isolation
was not so intense.
You go home to your cat
and your television,
the flickering light,
the gentle purring
your consolation and companion
deep into the night.
No last thoughts
before
you close your eyes
and drift away.

The Wedding Rehearsal

Two years old
ankles and knees
bounce to the
rhythm of rap.
Eyes round in
wonderment
at adults in
gold and glitter
bouncing to the
rhythm of rap.
Grandfather,
smile fixed
gaze locked
in wonderment
at all his children
bouncing to
the rhythm of rap.
Bride and groom
to be
seek his blessing
as the music fades
replaced by
the joyous notes
of love
in the hearts
of the
bride and groom
to be, who will then
dance to the rhythm of rap.

The Funeral

A raven cries
a note of anguish,
a myna, her cry of despair.
A pigeon coos,
mourning a lost love.
I am silent and empty,
all feeling wrenched away
into a void,
leaving a void,
so deep and so dark.

The cold, forbidding
stainless steel doors
open,
reveal the flames,
roaring,
waiting,
competing
with the silent anguish
and the deafening chant
of those left behind.

Belief, faith, love
and looming loneliness
bid a farewell
which nobody should have to.

The hesitant yet final turn away
from the now closed doors
stumbling with grief
on numb legs, barely supporting
numb mind and numb body,
helped by a caring, compassionate
circle of family and friends,
providing a crutch
which will have to be discarded
and life will have to go on,
never the same.
Never.

The House

Michelle leaned back against the pillows, pulled up her knees and propped the journal against them. Tracing the silver moon on the book's cover she looked around at her friends nestled into sleeping bags.

"Anyone want to hear a *funny* story?" she asked, blue eyes twinkling with mischief as her little sister settled into the corner. Grinning at the nods and knowing giggles from her friends, she turned her full attention to the journal.

The last paraglider from Marshall Peak descend out of view as Jen pulled open the door. The house sighed, engulfing her in the stale air and apprehension that was its presence. It was alive, or at least she felt it was. She sensed its eyes on her as if something watched from inside the walls.

She swallowed as she stepped over the threshold, determined to get through just one more night. Jen had lived in the house a month. And to ask her, it had been a month too long. But she forced a smile, it was all her imagination - she knew it. Still, she was uncomfortable enough that the house was back on the market.

The hair on her neck stood on end as she passed the silver framed mirror in the dining room. A shadow played at the edge of her vision, dancing into the mirror then out of sight as she turned to stare at her reflection. This happened every time she walked through the dining room. Every time she passed *that* mirror and she resolved to leave the cursed thing here.

The mirror had been covered when she'd viewed the house. It wasn't until she moved in that she saw the ornately detailed frame, curves giving the impression of waves cascading onto the surface. Jen knew nothing about antiques, but it looked expensive. It had been left by the previous owners, and the longer she lived here the more certain she was they purposely ignored her attempts to contact them.

Turning from the mirror, the feeling of being watched intensified. She forced herself not to look behind her. Deliberately she strode into the kitchen, keeping her back squared to the mirror. While her dinner heated, she poured Neutro into a bowl for Del.

Taking the personalized dog bowl to the back door, she glanced over her shoulder. Eyes trained on the mirror she pulled the patio door open and whistled.

Del raced across the lawn then froze at the threshhold, a deep growl issuing from him. White and black fur stood straight along the ridge of his back and he shivered all over. No matter how she coaxed, or what she promised, he would not step into the house.

Giving up as the microwave beeped, she set the bowl on the patio and turned back into the room. Picking up a journal she'd left by the door, she trained her gaze on the silver moon of the cover and she started past the mirror.

But the shadow commanded her attention. It danced at the corner of her vision, teasing, beckoning. Just before Jen had taken her fifth step, her head snapped around and her gaze locked with that of her reflection's.

For a split second her hazel eyes stared back. Then the surface shimmered, rippling from the center and her reflection disappeared. She was frozen to the spot, unable to move as the mirror bowed, pushing out of the frame. Silver fingers stretched towards her, closing around her shoulders.

The start of a scream pierced the night as silvery darkness surrounded her, drawing her towards the mirror. The last thing Jen heard was Del's frantic barking as she was pulled into the frame.

"That's not funny. Mom!" Sarah yelled as she slipped from her sleeping bag and ran down the hall towards her parent's bedroom.

The girls laughed as Michelle snapped the journal closed. She enjoyed scaring her sister, but she knew what would come now.

"What have I told you about frightening Sarah?" Her father's annoyance cut the laughter to muffled giggles.

Michelle looked up as the sleep glazed blue eyes of her father peered in and locked on hers.

"I can send everyone home, you know."

"Aw dad, she wouldn't go away. Besides, it's just a stupid story," Michelle said. Her icy stare drilled into Sarah who peeked in from behind their father's arm.

"It is not. You said it was in the journal." Sarah wiped the last of the tears her eyes.

"Regardless. Sarah, off to bed. And, you... Enough with the stories." Michelle's father yawned and shook his head as he herded Sarah towards her room.

Threat of punishment past, the girls lapsed into renewed giggles. Still, they buried their heads in their pillows to keep the sound from reaching the back of the house. The amusement subsided and Michelle got up.

"Ice cream?" she asked, as she strolled out of the den. Echoes of ascent followed her through the living room.

Michelle glanced at the silver mirror hanging on the wall and goose bumps sprang up on her arms. The journal she'd found in the coat closet made her uneasy about it. But she would never let anyone know, especially not Sarah.

Pulling the mint chocolate chip from the freezer and four spoons from the drawer, she headed back to the den. As she passed the mirror, a shadow danced at the edge of her vision. Her head snapped around and hazel eyes stared out at her. The image held up a pen for a moment before the surface rippled, blurring the image and continuing the waved pattern of the frame. As the image dissolved, the pen clattered to the floor.

Need A J-O-B

Many flies walked on the window as the man rinsed the last plate and turned off the water. He listened to Amy Winehouse on his Zune player. The song, *Some Unholy War*, made him think of his dog, the hundred pound pit-bull biting at flies on the kitchen floor.

Now that the dishes needed to dry, the time for the dog's walk had arrived, as it did every morning before the heat of the day prevented a comfortable stroll on the road through the desert. And so he opened the door to the distant hourglass sand hills with her in tow.

As he walked toward the hills, on that lone dirt road with the dog, the hills seemed to drift further away. On the left, in the open space of low shrubs where jack rabbits ran, the dog ran after them. On the right, a fence marked the property line.

The man needed a job. He'd been living on his Godmother's ranch for over two months, enough time to become comfortable with this morning ritual, and to see a wild tarantula. It walked on the road where he walked now. It walked with slow deliberate steps toward the abandoned village of junk trailers filled with skeletons from the past on the other side of the ridge a hundred yards ahead. The man's feet stopped, and he remembered standing over the spider as it raised a hairy leg as if to say hello. The man said goodbye.

He stood at the intersection of engraved roads reading a sign that advertised over 200 acres of desert ready for development. He turned around with the leash in hand, whistling for the dog to follow. As he walked back, he hit rocks on the ground with the leash as if it were a whip.

Back at the house, he began the next step in his schedule, looking for jobs on the internet. Applying for jobs on the internet had become a numbers game. He figured, the more jobs he applied for, the more interviews he'd get, and the more chances he'd have of finding a dream job.

It started with accounts on Monster.com, Careerbuilder.com, and Jobing.com. He'd look through the new job postings and upload his résumé to anything that looked interesting in the greater Los Angeles area. The greater Los Angeles, meaning anything from Ventura to Dana Point, to Barstow, akin to the Bermuda Triangle; a place where jobs existed and disappeared without a trace.

He applied for every job, no matter what qualifications they demanded. Undeterred, he clicked send for a job at Rolling Stone Magazine that paid almost $100,000 a year. With minor tweaks to his résumé and cover letter, he applied to another job paying $10 an hour at a warehouse. And he clicked send again to another job, and another five jobs, and to ten more jobs, and...

In December, he found himself working as a Driver Helper at UPS. He'd worked at UPS before, and felt disappointed that a new exciting career in Southern California eluded him. Why the big move? He could have stayed home. However, he needed the money. The good news, the driver he helped met him at the Silver Lakes Golf Complex outside of Victorville. It only took five minutes to drive there and he could pick up groceries for the ranch.

The name of the driver he helped: Jim, like Jim Morrison. Only this Jim had a more conservative look on life. Jim did not write poetry. Jim drove UPS trucks. Jim had been driving UPS trucks for nearly 20 years. Jim had a wife, children, friends, and a family. Jim felt thankful to have a Driver Helper with the increase in package volume over the Christmas peak season, the same as any other year.

The man enjoyed the job at UPS. It broke his routine, and allowed him to see the area in a different way as they drove through the neighborhoods. Some of the homes had personal touches, for example, one had been made to look like the Adam's Family house. Others could be described as mansions, where he would be required to buzz the doorbell to enter a golden gate entryway and then jog around a pool to the front door in order to deliver a package.

As they ate lunch at a park near the lake, the man looked around at the homes, the golf course, and the water shining in the winter sun, and he daydreamed of being Jim the UPS driver, of having a home on the golf course, being married to one of the local women, and having kids going to the Silver Lakes school. He could understand why people lived in this hidden oasis.

During one of these reveries at lunch, he got a call from New York, New York. Shari Rosen, of Rolling Stone Magazine, wanted to know if he still had an interest in the West Coast Sales Representative job. It would require him to fly up and down the West Coast to maintain accounts in major urban areas. The man felt as if Ed McMahon were calling to see if he still wanted the $10 million from the Publishers Clearing House.

He stood on the shores of the lake answering Ms. Rosen's questions. He had experience in these matters. He'd worked as an Account Manager for three-years at a major publishing company. This seemed like his time to shine. This job would make the moving gamble a success.

And then, Ms. Rosen asked about his experience with metrics. Metrics? Like the Matrix? No. Jim said "lunch is over". And the hourglass sand slipped through as the distant hills floated further away. In a week he'd be unemployed on Christmas Day.

The Storm

The banner announcing the Riverside Home Show flapped in the breeze, threatening to rip itself from the twin flag poles that stood like soldiers in front of the Riverside Convention Center. In every corner of the building, entertainers were putting the finishing touches on their booth, stacking their wares and getting order forms ready for the flood of potential customers that day.

"Attention retailers" came a call over the loudspeakers. "The Show will open in one minute."

Richard shifted the last of the boxes next to the back wall of his booth. When he sold one of his products, a new cleaning product made from the essence of oranges, he would hand off one of the full boxes to the customer rather than selling them the display item, as so many other vendors at this show did. He found it distasteful to send the customer home with a 'used' item, and did not understand why other retailers took advantage of their customers so. He glanced over at his neighbor, a fortune teller who had been with the Home Show nearly as long as he. She had started up the business as a way to fuel her hobbies, but could now make a decent living off the customers who came to her for advice in every city the show visited. Richard shook his head, wishing that his own product could rake in the same kind of profit as her tarot cards did.

"What do you think, Esme?" Richard asked. "Do you think it will be a good show for us this weekend?"

The fortune teller shifted in her chair, and assumed the pose of a deep trance. "They are coming like a storm." she murmured in a deep voice.

"And just what is that supposed to mean?" he asked.

"Just what I said: they are coming like a storm." she said, winking at him.

The sound of cheers signaled the beginning of the show as customers burst forward from the main entrance of the convention center. Door prizes were being handed out in plastic bags advertising the local newspaper. Customers snatched them up from the hands of the greeters like they held cash or valuable jewels. Richard knew that in this show they would receive little more than a newspaper (detailing show vendors, exhibits and classes), and a handful of freebie items such as pens and plastic water bottles. This show, however, the owners had decided to slip in something special: a long bread knife in a box that boasted that it could slice through an aluminum can as easily as a tomato. But in Richard's experience, this promise fell short, as he knew that the blade could not cut through melted butter on a hot July day.

With plastic bags of booty in hand, the people of the city descended upon the first exhibit like a plague of locusts. Some snatched the items off of the display, even though they were not 'freebies'. A sign posted at the bottom of the table stated as much, but Richard knew that expecting people to read and act like responsible citizens was impossible to ask of a show such as this. It drew the wrong kind of crowd: people looking to get something for nothing. They argued when you refused to barter with them and stole something as often as not when your back was turned.

Richard turned away from the flood of people and looked to his own booth, trying to keep a faithful watch over his product, lest the human seagulls pillage his booth before he could make a single sale.

By the middle of the day, both Richard and Esme had made their booth fee, though it had cost them in both product and endurance. Richard had found himself wooing his customers with a spiel that sounded both corny and contrived, but he had sold two cases of the orange based cleaning product and only lost one of his three sample bottles thus far.

He pulled a fresh bottle out of the box and wrote: SAMPLE, PLEASE DO NOT TAKE across it in permanent marker. "So how did you fare, dear palm reader?" he asked his neighbor.

"I'm twenty dollars over the cost of the booth, but the third customer of the day stole my 'divining' rock."

"Ouch." Richard sympathized; in the past he had personal items taken from his booth when he was not watching, like a cell phone and the jacket to his suit. But he still could not understand the customer who had taken the tennis shoes that he had kept under his table to change into at the end of the night. His good dress shoes he could understand. But these old sneakers were on their last leg, so to speak. Why would anyone want someone's old gym shoes?

"It didn't cost much, though, and I can get a replacement easily enough."

"Really?" Richard asked.

"Yeah, I'll just have you keep an eye on my booth long enough to go back to Tiki God Gifts and buy another bag of them."

"Wait -what?"

"They're just the rocks people put in their fire pits, after all." Esme laughed. "She must have really felt like she was getting away with some-think big. And considering that she paid me forty bucks for a reading

94

while she stole a rock not even worth four dollars, I think I can live with it."

The two of them laughed over the little joke, which was quickly interrupted by a rumbling. "Did you hear that?" Richard asked her, craning his head towards the source of the disturbance. "It sounds like a thunderstorm."

"Yeah, but inside the building?" Esme asked.

The sound came closer, a thrumming noise which vibrated through their chests, locking the air in their lungs from fear. Soon the air around them darkened as they were surrounded by thousands upon thousands of buzzing bodies. The swarm moved throughout the building, passing customers and vendors without any notice and came to a stop nearest the endmost booth.

"Were those-?" Esme began to ask.

"Bees." Richard finished. He stood on his tiptoes to get a better look at the booth that had gotten the attention of the bees. It was a product that he had been introduced to at the same time he had settled his attention on his citrus cleaner. "I'm so glad that I decided to pass on that natural wax furniture polish."

"I agree, but who could have seen that coming?" Esme asked.

"You did, when you were in your trance this morning."

"I said that 'they are coming like a storm' -not 'swarm'."

"Close enough in my book."

Flying Cockroaches and Wild Lightning Storms

And so it was a thunderstorm that etched lightning in the sky and flooded the streets of El Barrio Cuchillo, which caused the power to go out. Lightning entangled the sky as my family poured outside. They were drawn to the lightning like the gnats that circle the hanging bulb in the back cuarto of my nana and tata's house. Down the street, house to house, an entire block of familia. Each door squeaked open on old hinges, as we were called to the powerful display of nature.

It was the first summer I stayed alone in Blythe, the small desert town where my mother grew up. A place I never really believed people should live, assuming the heat, or lack of sufficient shopping or even a hospital should have forced people out. But Tata promised that he'd teach me card games—the ones I'd watch him play alone at the kitchen table with neatly formed rows and decks, the ones his dad taught him after tireless days working at the mine. And Nana added that she'd supply me with enough saladitos and twenty five cent pickles from Westside Market to last me the summer. So, even though it started as a family visit, I stayed behind, biting my bottom lip and waving hesitantly to my parents as they drove the nine hours back to Fresno, without me.

I stayed with my nana and tata in the last house on the block, but the first house built in El Barrio Cuchillo, closest to the canal, where my cousins used to tell me (holding back giggles) that La Llorona walked at night. The slightly tilted but portly house was built by my great grandfather who insisted on building it below ground to withstand the sweltering summers in Blythe. So hot, my tio woke me up one morning to show me that he could fry an egg on the street. And it worked. As did the low set home which only had a single water cooler yet managed to stay cold during the 125 degree days of summer. Doors closed, lights out, and rags tucked in cracks to keep the cool air in. Nana would sit and do her wordsearch puzzles to the light of novellas on T.V., her glasses reflecting dramatic scenes of love quarrels.

But now it was night, and I had decided to go with my cousins three doors down, coaxed by the promise of card games, soda, and staying up all night wrapped in sleeping bags. As the storm roared, I became terrified by the unknown desert landscape, which shook my tia's old house with thunder, and lit up the sky like the strobe lights my cousins used to breakdance with. I felt my belly fill with fear, and my eyes began to sting from holding back tears in the face of my cousins who were used to this sort of thing. We continued playing our card game until Tia called us outside.

A pool of figures stood in the distance at the driveway of Nana and Tata's house, holding an assortment of pots, aluminum tins used for washing dogs, ice chests, clay water jugs, anything that could hold water. As we got closer to the house, I could see the look of terror on my nana's tired face as water swallowed her feet. The house had flooded, as it did every summer during these storms, and it made sense now why the house always smelled like mold, the tell-tale signs of tea colored water stains on the walls.

All the tios entered the house with large vessels as we took our place at Tata's command in a straight line from the living room—from tallest to shortest—out of the front gate of the garden, and into the street. I struggled to find my place, stepping on feet, and splashing water on legs in the dark. Then, starting in a heavy stream from deep in the darkness of the house the water came pouring from one tub to the next. It spilled in rhythm as they poured from side to side into each other's container--some slipping from the quick movement and hitting the water below, a single note in a song. We became a waterfall, releasing water into the asphalt river. I stood silenced for a moment, awed by the display—by the act of community I would never see back home in Fresno. I imagined the house being built in this fashion so many years ago. A line of family members, carting adobe bricks from hand to hand to form the structure.

"Apurate mija," Tata said, catching me daydreaming, my impatient cousin emptying water at my feet. I was at the end of the line, in the middle of the deserted street, with a rusted coffee can my tata stored out back, for no particular purpose or maybe this very purpose. That's how Tata was, he saved things, and even if he hadn't done it for a reason at the time, he always found one.

The rain slowly turned into a drizzle which made the air thick and hard to breathe. We worked for hours through the night, listening to the music we created with water until the sun peaked over the canal at the end of the street and the house was finally rid of water. The air thinned, our bodies weakened and the sun revealed that we were covered in mud. The brand new jumper my mom bought for my summer stay was ruined and I was excited about it. I had never experienced such adventure back home; my clothes never had a story to tell other than spilled soup or a mishap with a ketchup packet. This was a story I could tell my friends when I returned home, still high off salty treats and lightning flashes, flailing my hands and showing them the motion in which we all joined together to keep the water out of the house.

My nana corralled all of the young cousins and took us to the restroom behind the house, built outdoors because my great grandfather thought it unsanitary to have one inside. It was perfect for these situations, but terrible in the middle of the night, clearing lagañas and stumbling over rocks, the pet goose waiting in silence. The large shower, fitted with two shower heads, fit my five cousins and I all at once. We crowded in like cattle and as my nana adjusted the temperature, a cockroach fluttered about blindly, and then flew through a hole in the cracked wall. I wasn't afraid anymore. I was getting used to these sorts of adventures in Blythe—flying cockroaches, wild lightning storms, being chased by the roaming goose in the backyard.

After we washed our bodies off, fully clothed, we laid on the concrete. The dry heat of the day had already settled into town and penetrated the concrete, distorting the street and waving bodies in the distance. We spread out on the concrete like dates and let the sun dry us from above and below. And rested for a fleeting moment before someone shouted out "tag you're it" and we all hopped to our feet again and scattered in the street, leaving our wetness behind, a united form of moisture that looked like we left behind our shadows because we all got up so fast. Nana heard the ruckus and stood at the squeaking screened door demanding we get some sleep. We all scattered again.

I stayed to help her dry rugs and mop. We set up enough borrowed fans throughout the house that we ran out of outlets. We opened up every door and window letting light inside, and for the first time that summer I could actually see the misshapen walls and mismatched furniture. I laid on the bed, which once belonged to my mom, and fell into a trance, hypnotized by the humming of fans and the sweet chirp of birds outside.

The house felt bright and the heat warmed and calmed my excited nerves. I wondered if this was how my mom felt waking up in this house every morning. Or, if she hated the heat, waking up to the weary crow of the rooster out back and the smell of wet dirt outside the window after the rain. Maybe that's why we rarely came back here.

When I fell asleep, I dreamt of a childhood in El Barrio Cuchillo, surrounded by family and so close to nature, so different from city life back home, where I feared everything that lay beyond the four walls of my house, and sometimes what was within them. I dreamt of playing hopscotch on the sidewalk with my cousins, fishing with my tio in the canal, feeding the hens in the morning and the thrill of finding a newly hatched egg. I dreamt of bonfires out back, giggling with my cousins as Tata played the guitarra and my tios drank cheap beer and sang to the music. I dreamt of pitch black desert skies, the buzz of chicharras, stars that invite you into the universe, and the sweet smell of the earth, the tierra that lay just outside the door.

MICHELLE GONZALEZ

Midnight Drives

On our third, of many, dates
we drove down the 60 freeway
around the midnight hour
to see the glimmering meteors.
We talked about how
beautiful the sky would look
once we got to the Badlands,
small but still narrow.
I imagined it would look like
a brighter version of the moon,
glowing in the darkness
all alone.

We passed the exits with the stores
and other signs of life,
until we reached our destination.
The headlights lead the way
to the dark hidden spot.

We got out of the car and
sat on his dusty hood,
looking up all we saw were
the shadows of clouds
covering the dark sky.
There were no meteors to be seen;
somehow that was fine with us.
We decided to stay and talk awhile.
He asked, "Have you ever made a wish,
on a shooting star?"
I lie and say, "No."
It's too early to tell
all my secrets.

Spiritual Journey to Mt Rubidoux

Hiking all the way to the cross
is as close as I have ever come
to touching the clouds.
I could hardly feel my feet
as I passed the one mile mark.
I gasped for air
but my chest felt like it could not open.
Every few feet, I stopped to rest
which turned out to be
a mistake as my legs ached even more.
The sun beats on us as
I prayed for a breeze.
I sat on the huge grey rock
beneath the cross;
my mind went blank.
I thought of nothing else
but the clear sky and fresh air
on this not so smoggy day
and I know,
someday I will return.

Starbucks on 3rd and Market

"Push the button,
push the damn button,"
is what I hear as I sit
on the cold patio.
Interesting characters cross
my path at 10' o clock
on a Saturday night.
I resist the urge
to grab my purse and hold
it tight.
Thoughts cross my mind
like how can I be downtown
and in the wrong part of town
at the same time?
The distant lights of the Mission Inn
put me at ease
as I remember walking around
the festival of lights
holding a hot cup of hot chocolate
and it brings me back
to the noises and sounds
of 3rd and Market.

JOAN KOERPER

Illumination at The Mission Inn:
The Transcontinental Transformation
of Mary Chase Perry Stratton

Suddenly, flickering candles dim in the parlor. Incense billows from bowls of desert sand. My fingers, lightly resting on the rounded edge of the flat-top begin to tremble in unison with the tables' shaking in unpredictable movement until, abruptly, everything is still. The medium, Moira McLaughlin, speaks in the soft, sweet voices of my mother and sister who both perished in the flu epidemic of 1913. The tones and cadence of their utterances reverberate in every cell of my body as I begin to shiver. My breath stops short, resuming only in minute, rapid, short bursts of life. Their deaths precipitated a nervous breakdown from which it took me three years to recover. I stay strong, but, little do I suspect, this is just the beginning...

How did a level-headed ceramicist end up in a séance at the Glenwood Mission Inn in Riverside, California, you ask? My story has been untold, until now. Perhaps that reticence has been in err. You decide.

My adventures commenced with an odd request accompanying Mr. Frank Miller's commission for my hand-made tiles wherein he insisted I escort the shipment on an all expense paid trip and supervise an installation of a St. Francis of Assisi fountain at his hotel. A sizeable commitment in 1919 when you consider this required traveling by Transcontinental Railroad from Pewabic Pottery in Detroit, Michigan to The Glenwood Mission Inn in Riverside, California. The Great War had just ended, the world was still recovering from the flu pandemic of 1918, my dear friend and mentor Charles Freer was in ill health, I had been married only a year and business at my pottery was brisk. The timing of Mr. Miller's request was impertinent at best, but with my husband's encouragement, I accepted.

I was no stranger to stories of California. Like thousands of other men, my father, William Walbridge Perry, joined the frenzy of the 1850's Gold Rush. His fireside tales, however, paled in light of the illuminating experiences that unfolded on my journey; a tapestry entwining the clay of the earth, and my soul, the story of the 'Far Away' people told me by Chief Francisco Patencio, an Agua Caliente Cahuilla Indian leader and a séance at The Glenwood Mission Inn.

My name is Mary Chase Perry Stratton. I was born in 1867 in the Upper Peninsula of Michigan, in Hancock, a copper producing area rich in clay. As a child, I loved digging up clay, shaping it into figures and designs and firing it in a brick kiln. Colors and art captured me. Later, I lived in Asheville, North Carolina, Ann Arbor and Detroit and studied china painting and sculpture at the Art Academy of Cincinnati when I was twenty. Ohio, you remember, was really the center of the pottery Arts and Crafts movement at that time, and I was exposed to many outstanding potters and potteries as well before studying at the Art Museum in Detroit where I met Mary Elizabeth Higgins.

By the age of 26, in 1893, when I put on my first formal exhibition at the World's Fair in Chicago, I was considered one of the leaders in the art of china painting, had a studio in Asheville, was creating and selling my wares, giving lessons, and writing for numerous publications on the subject.

When I returned to Detroit to continue studies and open a studio, one of my neighbors was Horace Caulkins, a dentist, who made false teeth from porcelain. He developed the Revelation Kiln to heat the porcelain in 1892. I saw that the kiln also held many possibilities for ceramicists of artistic mediums. We became business partners to promote the kiln and I traveled extensively in the East and Mid-West, demonstrating china painting and endorsing the Revelation Kilns to artists as they were becoming the standard in the field.

Eventually, feeling I had exhausted the medium of china painting, I re-focused my energies and career on ceramics. On October 8, 1903, Caulkins and I formed another business partnership, opening the "Stable Workshop" in an abandoned stable. We started out with small, saleable items such as bowls and vases. I confess right off I was not truly proficient at throwing on the wheel and hired Joseph Herrick, a trained pot thrower. My forte was making glazes and glazing, decorating, handbuilding and designing tiles. Even before our doors opened, we had a commission for $1,000 worth of bowls and lamp jars from Burley and Company of Chicago, Illinois.

We ventured into architectural ceramics, when architect William Buck Stratton, commissioned us to make handmade tiles for a residential fireplace surround. The tiles were very well accepted and other orders soon flowed in. Needing more space, we hired William Stratton to design and build a new pottery.

In 1905, I named the studio Pewabic Pottery. I loved the name. Not only did I traverse the Pewabic mines with my father, who was a medical doctor for the Pewabic Mine, among others, Pewabic, in Chippewa, means copper-colored clay. It was perfect. A year later, Stratton, Caulkins and I were founding members of the Detroit Society of Arts and Crafts. The new pottery opened in 1907 and the lamps, vases, bottles and tiles were selling well.

After many years of experimenting with my own glaze formulas and glazes, in the Spring of 1909, I removed a simple piece from the kiln and the iridescent glaze was everything I had hoped for and unlike anything I had ever seen. I was even offered one hundred dollars for that three inch by one and one-half inch vase and refused it. This was the beginning of a new era and the cornerstone of the demand for Pewabic tile and wares.

Perhaps you have visited the Smithsonian? My wares have been on display there in the Charles Lang Freer Art Gallery since 1923. Or, perhaps you have seen my installations at the Detroit Public Library, the State Capitol Building in Lincoln NE, many locations on the Michigan State University campus, and The National Shrine of the Immaculate Conception in Washington DC. My hand-made tiles are installed in hundreds, if not thousands, of residences and businesses in the United States, as well as schools, libraries, museums, monuments and churches all over the United States, and my work is in museums worldwide.

In any case, it was the popularity of my iridescent glazed tiles that inspired a commission by Frank Miller, owner of The Glenwood Mission Inn in Riverside, CA. If I remember correctly, it was William B. Stratton, the architect who designed Pewabic Pottery, and much later became my husband, who told Arthur Benton, the original architect of the Glenwood Mission Inn, about my pottery...although Mr. Miller may have found out about it in a number of ways. Henry Ford and his family, for instance, visited the Glenwood in 1913. And, I understand Mr. Miller was at some of the World's Fairs and I exhibited my wares at each from 1893-1950's.

Michigan, as you may or may not know, is a virtual compendium of Native American names and pottery, especially at the mysterious Indian Mounds. Making plans to visit Native American lands and tribes in New Mexico and Arizona en route, I packed some of my own pieces as presents for Native potters and was readily able to establish rapport via this ancient art. We are potters, creators, artists; citizens of the world.

Arriving at my last stop, the Cahuilla reservation, near Agua Caliente (Palm Springs), California, nestled at the base of Mt. San Jacinto rising 10,834 feet above sea level, desert at the bottom, alpine at the top, I was awed. I was greeted amiably but with some reserve by Cahuilla elder Francisco Patencio, a thin man of short stature with jet black hair parted on the side, deep creases running from each side of his nose to his chin and large ears, who held his head high and walked with a sense of pride. The Cahuilla are a hard working and industrious people.

I was taken to observe a pot being fired. Their utilitarian pottery holds true to the philosophy of the Arts and Crafts Movement, although it was unknown to them. Indeed, Maria Martinez, a Tewa potter in New Mexico explained to me that there is no word in Native languages to designate "art" as something separate from Life. It is an inherent practice to walk in, and instill, beauty in every object made. I watched, studying all the stages of Cahuilla pot making: the clay being ground into a fine powder; water being added to it to reach the desired consistency for rolling the coils, pressing the coils into the preferred shape, smoothing them on the inside with a small stone and, on the outside with a wooden paddle. Afterward, the pot is baked in the sun for a day and burned on a fire for one day. The result? Thin-walled, red, cooking pots, water jars, parching trays, storage jars, ladles and pipes characterized by incised zig-zag and diamond-shaped patterns.

It is the basketry, however, that is outstanding, for Cahuilla women are among the finest basketmakers in the world and a Cahuilla wife enhances her social prestige considerably if she is a notable basketmaker. The baskets…"coiled" or sewn, made on a multiple foundation of a type of grass, have beautiful designs taken from the environment; lightening, waterdog, clouds, animals. I was invited to sit and watch Mrs. Martinez use only an awl, made from the leg bone of a deer or a long cactus needle set in a wooden handle to achieve this meticulous process.

In an extraordinary move, Chief Patencio offered to take me to a site, used for sacred rituals, to see the petroglyphs (rock carvings) and rock paintings, called pictographs, that inspire the designs on their pottery and basketry. Climbing up the rocks to the right of the stream in Murray Canyon, we arrived at an outcrop of a boulder with a small cavelike space underneath. Crawling in, we sat quietly. A deep sense of protected, cool, comfort enveloped me in this sacred space. After a time, the Chief pointed to the diamond-shaped paintings and zig-zag patterns on the ceiling and, gently, nodding his head, he said, "I will tell you the story of the Far Away Ones". He began.

"The Far Away Ones called themselves, *Mo moh pechem*, or 'moaning in pain' and lived in the mountains. They came before us," the Chief told me, his voice flowing; lilt, tone and intonation almost hypnotizing, "and we know very little about them, but they were people who had families… only they had much more power and, after long prayer, could fly. Only then did the power come. Much of the time they stayed in one place and then, when it came time, they flew away again." They flew to each mountain and named it. Mt. San Jacinto they named *I a kitch*, meaning "smooth cliffs" and they stayed there a long time. It is said that the head of the tribe went against a traditional custom and was killed by a mountain lion. Then, the tribe walked down the mountainside to Palm Canyon, but another leader did not want to go further and turned himself into a rock. He is there still. The people flew to San Felipe Valley and stayed there and raised large families. Because they lost their leaders, their power weakened, eventually leaving them forever."

The coach swayed in mesmerizing rhythm, wheels clicking and clacking, speeding through the desert, west toward Riverside. Similarly, Chief Patencio's spellbinding story replayed in my mind, matching the measure and cadence of the trains' progression. His words spinning images in my head, summoning faint recollections of other tales I heard as a child in Michigan and the offerings to the kiln gods I put in every load of pottery I fire. Pressing my face against the train car window, I merged with the vast open spaces, and millions of stars. Was this simply a fantastical story? Or, something else? What if the original peoples came from another place...a planet? What if we could fly? What if the veil is thin, like the walls of a Cahuilla pot, between time and space, what has come before, what is now, and what is to come?

Mr. Miller's jovial brother, Ed, picked me up at the train depot in one of the Mission Inn's fleet of Stearn-Knights automobiles and we began our short drive to the Inn already in view. I exercised amenities and good manners when I complimented the effort. In reality, expecting an architecturally consistent structure, I was caught completely off guard by the eclectic configuration. Surveying the exterior, I viewed influences, designs and styles from Mission Revival, Spanish Gothic, Spanish Colonial Revival, Mediterranean Revival and Moorish Revival architecture.

"Mi casa es su casa" Mr. Miller said, graciously greeting me with his wife Marion and sister Alice Richardson, who managed the hotel. My bags were carried by William James Herbert to my room while Mr. Miller took me on a personal tour of the Inn.

"Our first paying customer was in 1875 and I bought the hotel from my father in 1880," Mr. Miller explained. "As you can see, I have made many changes and additions since then, determined to establish a world class hotel to accompany our growth and appeal. I'm sure you know that in 1895, Riverside boasted the highest income per capita in the United States and we were able to maintain that distinction for many years. But, I am getting off the mark here. I am aware that you and Mr. Caulkins were incorporators of the Detroit Museum of Art, and, of course, Mr. Stratton is an architect, thus, I know you are more interested in the art and architecture of the hotel so let me start there.

"Forgive me. I have the description of the Inn etched in my memory from one of the original announcements I wrote, and sometimes can't seem to move beyond it, Mrs. Stratton. You will see that we began the

Glenwood with a structure that is 'a long, low, cloistered building of the Mission type, enclosing a spacious court surrounded by magnificent old trees and palms which adjoins the stately Campanile with its sweet chime of old Mission bells.' On the third floor is the beautiful Paseo de las Palmas, a promenade seven hundred feet long, and a grand court with its grape-arbored Pergola. You can also see the solarium, or sun parlor, cloistered corridors, a Patio, or inner court, along with heavy opened-timbered ceilings throughout the Inn, and massive chimneys. I am incorporating elements of all twenty-one California Missions, you know. There is, of course, the music room and the St. Cecilia stained glass window with the face of my beloved first wife, Isabella, instead of the image of St. Cecilia. And, the St. Francis stained glass window with my face instead of St. Francis'. How I love these windows!" he said enthusiastically.

I nodded, biting the inner side of my left lip, restraining comment. Quite honestly, hardly a Roman Catholic, I was somewhat appalled at the idea of inserting a portrait of oneself for a saint, although, come to think of it, perhaps many of us are trying to emulate their best qualities? Nonetheless, it left a sour taste in my mouth.

The tour continued through the intricately built and complicated structure with exterior arcades, narrow passageways and numerous patios looking at castle towers, minarets, flying buttresses, and Mediterranean domes in a building which consumes an entire block. The view from the Spanish roof garden was exquisite, I must say; the San Gorgonio and San Gabriel Mountains are a stunning backdrop.

Mr. Miller continued, "….the building is fire-proof, steam heated, all the chambers are suites, with baths, and we have long distance telephone so you can talk with your husband whenever you wish.

Lastly, we have arrived at your lodgings for the duration of your stay. I thought you might enjoy this room the most. This is the in Cloister Wing which was designed by architect Arthur Benton," Mr. Miller announced as he swung open the door.

Running my hand across the handmade Limbert dresser, I let out a long sigh of relief. While the Mission Revival Movement in California is considered by some an outgrowth of the Arts and Crafts Movement, relatively quickly upon my arrival, I was able to see the evidence that distinguishes the two…at least for a purist like me. The Arts and Crafts Movement, inspired by the social reform movement, embodies a philosophy that individually designed beautiful handmade wares such as pottery, woodcraft and buildings, somehow capture and contain the creative spirit of the artist; that they enhance people's lives while resulting from decent employment for the craftsmen working in good conditions.

This belief was in direct contrast to the soulless mass production practices of the Victorian period. The Mission Revival Movement in California, however, had no relation to the social reform movement. Rather, it was sentimental; an architectural and decorative movement with literary overtones.

The quarters greatly appealed to my Arts and Crafts soul. "You are correct, Mr. Miller. Charles Limbert, as you know, is from Holland and Grand Rapids, Michigan. I have met him on many occasions and commissioned numerous handmade pieces from him for Pewabic and my home. Ah...and this chair is handcrafted by Gustav Stickley. Again, I have several of his pieces in my home. And, I deeply admire the Van Briggle pottery. His matte glaze is the opposite of that I produce, but the glazes he created were thought lost to time. I met him, you know, when we studied in Cincinnati. He also worked at Rookwood Pottery. He was an Arts and Crafts purist as am I. What a loss that he died of tuberculosis at such a young age. Thank you, Mr. Miller. These accommodations are lovely."

Alone, closing my eyes, I tried to sort out the juxtapositions in my surroundings. Mr. Miller was entranced by the Missions, but there was never a Mission in the Riverside, San Bernardino area...the closest being Mission San Luis Rey in San Diego County, or the Mission San Gabriel. He was not Catholic, yet hailed the Saints, particularly St. Francis and St. Cecilia, feeling free to exercise license and substitute he and his wife in the reproductions of their images. I thought of the Cahuillas and other Native American tribes who were forced into labor or decimated by illness from contact with the Spanish who established the missions and were further devastated when Mexico destroyed the mission system long before the U.S. came into California in 1846, although the ruination continued. My heart went out to them. Outside of the Stickley and Limbert furniture, and the Van Briggle pottery, I saw little art or ceramics from America. On the other hand, Mr. Miller was a congenial and most competent hotelier, doing a splendid job of acquiring art from Europe, the Orient, and Mexico, during his travels to bring to the people of Riverside and, indeed, the world since industrialists and world leaders gathered here for Peace Conferences and more. Such contradictions.

After a morning of supervising the installation, nearing completion, Mr. Miller suggested three other guests, including Moira McLaughlin visiting from Summerland, California, and I take an excursion to the top of Mt. Rubidoux. Excusing William James Herbert from his doorman duties to be our personal guide and driver, Mr. Miller waved us off. Sitting within a mile of the Inn, the auto easily ascended the smooth, black-topped road to the top of the 1,329 foot mountain. There stood a large wooden cross, easily seen from a distance of miles, giving testament to the religious preference of the owner of the land; Mr. Miller. It had already become a tradition for like-minded souls to walk up the hill on Easter Sunday morning for sunrise services at the cross.

The clarity of the three hundred and sixty degree view of the terrain from the pinnacle is truly spectacular. I was most refreshed and renewed by the sight of the surrounding mountain peaks; San Gabriel, San Gorgonio, San Jacinto, and San Bernardino, most still gracing a mantle of snow, vast expanses of orange groves, the city, nearby settlements and the Santa Ana River which borders Riverside both north and west. Descending the hill, we drove approximately a mile to the north, into Fairmount Park, an assigned expanse of property on the Santa Ana Riverbed. Stopping in the shade at Evans Lake, we enjoyed the flocks of ducks and birds also taking respite not far from the Riverside Lawn Bowling Clubhouse.

Smoothing a fallen leaf in her hands, Moira McLaughlin looked at me inquiringly. Melodically, her Irish brogue queried, "Do you believe in spiritualism, Mary Chase?" I lived by no religious creed. My life embodies the philosophy and spirit of the Arts and Crafts Movement. My silence and raised eyebrows only spurred her on. "It is a philosophy and religion of continuous life. We're not atheists, you know, we do believe in God. I am a medium, and communicate with those who live in the spirit world. In my city, Summerland, near Santa Barbara, the center of town is a séance gathering place." When I gave her no response, she continued. "You know that Eliza Tibbets, also a Mid-Westerner…she was born in Minnesota…received and planted the first two navel oranges in Riverside, thereupon triggering a new kind of California gold. Well, she was a well-known and competent Spiritualist medium. And, although many people tend to forget, Dr. James P. Greves, who co-established the colony of Riverside from your fair state of Michigan was also a spiritualist. So were some of the thirty people from Michigan who accompanied him here to locate the colony. Even John North, also credited for co-establishing the colony of Riverside, hosted séances in his home in Minnesota and here in Riverside. Please, why don't you come tonight to my room? I am holding a séance. You will be in good company. Most of the men will be over in Chinatown, gambling or cavorting. Lord knows, there is no liquor to be had legally. Even if there were, Mr. Miller won't have it in the Inn. We will have some time to ourselves."

Our two companions were squealing in consensual excitement, nodding their heads yes with delight, while I stayed still. In time, however, after Moira Ann McLaughlin agreed to let me investigate the room both before and after the séance for any "traps" or tricks, I acquiesced. At 9pm, I knocked on her room door.

I left the séance reeling, hurriedly seeking the safety of my ample room in the Cloister Wing where I felt most at home. Rushing straight to the high arched window, I drew back the curtains, flipped open the latch of the casement and pulled it forward, trembling hands clutching each sash trying to regain my balance, inhaling the fresh air into the deepest parts of my lungs. My mind was spinning. I had communicated with my mother and sister. It was not a side show. It was real. Their voices continued to sing in my head; the conversation replayed verbatim; a phonograph record stuck on repeat. One minute I was pacing back and forth, the next, bending forward simply trying to get my breath. Despite efforts to steady myself by focusing on glazing recipes, it was well into the night before I fell asleep.

I am aroused to a half-awakened state when the backside of my left hand strikes my forehead unsuccessfully trying to shield my eyes peering through a kiln peephole from the glowing wares of my dream when the light accelerated. But, I am not dreaming at all. Instead, my room is filled with a brilliant light. I jolt to a sitting position balancing myself with my hands on either side of me on the bed. A glowing human shaped figure stands inside the window, to the left of my foot board. Motionless, my eyes dart back and forth, up and down, across the room searching every nook and cranny for an explanation…evidence of a hoax. But, there is no source of light outside the window projecting the figure into the room. Nor is there any light emanating from anywhere else in the room. The figure generates its own force field and I squint, trying to protect my eyes from the brightness. While the figure is transparent, I catch sight of zig zag patterns on its' left shoulder and diamond shaped markings running down its right leg. Quite unexpectedly, in a nano-second of vague recognition, I feel my shoulders drop, exhaling a long, low, panic-trapped breath.

The figure speaks.

"You, who honor earth, air, fire and water, you know who we are. Chief Patencio told you about us. You listened. You respected our sacred cave and are thinking about us; taking our legend and lessons seriously. Your people have not listened to the stories of the ancient ones; disregarding the words of the original peoples, the Far Away People.

I have been sent to tell you more but only if you agree to tell no one while you are alive. And even afterward, only with our permission."

Every cell in my body is responding. My lips turn upward, smiling and I feel my eyes dancing.

"I vow I will speak of this to no one. Please? Continue?" I ask.

The figure's head nods in agreement. I settle in to listen.

Returning home with a reassurance still hard for me to fathom, I continued my lifelong commitment to the philosophy, spirit and work of the Arts and Crafts Movement at my Pewabic Pottery, my credo being, "Simple shapes live throughout the ages." In 1921 I was awarded the prestigious Logan Medal at the Exhibition of Applied Arts at Chicago's Art Institute and in 1930 the University of Michigan awarded me an honorary Master of Arts degree for many contributions as an artist, innovator, and craftsman in the field of ceramic art. Three years later, in 1933, Wayne State University, in Detroit, bestowed me an honorary Doctor of Science degree in recognition of my research in chemicals and glazes.

When my husband died, on May 12, 1938, following a streetcar accident, I went to San Diego to recuperate and re-visited the Glenwood Mission Inn on my way home. It was not the same, as Mr. Miller died in 1935, but I was deeply comforted by the stopover at such a time of sorrow and loss. Twelve years later, in 1947, I was awarded the highest tribute in the ceramics industry....the Charles Fergus Binns Medal, named for Alfred University's first director of ceramics.

I worked in the studio until I died, the day after my ninety-fourth birthday in 1961. I left many glaze recipes for the potters who continue my tradition at Pewabic. Some formulas, however, admittedly my best, actually, I took with me. No one has been able to recreate those glazes since. To me, it is each potter's journey to make their own glazes. Similarly, I still cannot tell you all that I learned on my first trip to the Glenwood Mission Inn, or that I have learned since. In the web of life, each of us is clay and space experimenting with relationships; juggling chemicals, heat, time and energy to produce the colors that uncover and illuminate our essence. Pewabic is still operating, and, I am proud to say that like the Mission Inn, it is a National Historic Landmark.

If you would like something tangible, representing both the spirit of the Arts and Crafts Movement, the Mission Inn and Riverside, I encourage you to consider a handmade tile by Riverside potter Kelly Noble, or a piece by Ed Traynor, who also studied at the Cranbrook Academy of Art in Michigan.

However, if you would like an intangible experience, I invite you to look very carefully upon the walkways, passages, rooms, windows and down into the catacombs of the Mission Inn. There you may catch a glimpse of me, iridescent and luster colors appearing where there is only space, or a whiff of Michigan clay, lovingly visiting the place I first awakened to truths that stretched the clay of my soul beyond time and to the farthest galaxies. I assure you, I will not be alone.

Authors note: Even short stories often require acknowledgements, especially when extensive inquiries and investigation are necessary to ensure historical accuracy. While Frank Miller did not commission Mary Chase Perry Stratton's tiles for the Mission Inn, and the two, to my knowledge never met, the facts in this story concerning the characters, the Mission Inn, Pewabic Pottery, Chief Patencio, the Cahuilla, pottery types and style, and the Arts and Crafts Movement are accurate. The author is deeply indebted to the following, without whose assistance, this story would have never reached the kiln: Steve Lech, President of the Riverside County Historical Association, Hanna Neilson, Archivist, Pewabic Pottery, Detroit, Michigan, Steve Spiller and the staff of the Mission Inn Museum and Patricia Majher, editor of Michigan History Magazine, a publication of the Historical Society of Michigan. And, to Ruth Nolan, poet and educator, who suggested the "Mission Inn Project", hurling me into a frenzy of research and unchartered territory with my writing. Last, but never least, to my readers, Deenaz Coachbuilder, Jean Waggoner, Amy Floyd, speakerofstones, and Mike Cluff, who compel me to be the best writer I can be. On the personal side, I am a graduate of Michigan State University where Pewabic Pottery tiles grace not only numerous sites on campus, but buildings and churches I frequented in Detroit and throughout Michigan growing up. Most likely, the vas and china painted plates in my cabinet, delicately and painstakingly decorated by my maternal grandmother, Mary Elizabeth Higgins Burrell were a result of taking china painting classes from Mary Chase Perry. My father, musician and educator William Koerper had numerous connections with Pewabic Pottery. I rode by Pewabic Pottery as detective with the Detroit Police Department oblivious to its historical significance while being immersed in the beauty it produced in my environment. As a writer and potter with deep roots in Michigan and California, and a twenty-seven year resident of the Inland Empire, enjoying the environs of the Mission Inn, writing this story was deeply personal and a sincere privilege.

MacArthur Park Rock

"Watch out below," I holler, peering over the balcony railing of the Riverside Community College Ceramics/Sculpture building perched halfway down a canyon in the heart of Riverside, California. The white object in my outstretched arms, raised above my head, is about to be heaved three stories down onto the pavement.

"What are you doing?" my professor, John Hopkins, queries.

"Sculpting," I respond.

"Is that what you call it?" he replies, turning back into the studio.

Frankly, I have no clue. I was driven to this desperate measure when, despite all efforts to avoid taking sculpture, I'm in class attempting non-representational three dimensional figures. Pottery on the wheel is a joyous spiritual experience for me and I take great pleasure in calling forth hand-built turtles and goddesses, but, I am completely intimidated by sculpture. When John announces the purpose of the class is to help students understand three dimensions, not figures, I know I'm sunk.

The white rectangle of plaster stands before me, awaiting my efforts to transform it into a piece of art, as if it already knows the battle horns have sounded. I just didn't hear them.

Metal carving tools bounce off the solid mass making eerie clinking sounds as they hit the floor. My Black and Decker hand-held electric drill shimmies and shakes dancing on an immovable surface. Donning my facemask and apron, bearing the appearance of a mutant bug, I work with my light, cordless, hand-held Dremel drill when it freezes, irreparably destroyed by plaster dust. Resentfully, I toss it in the trash.

Completely entertained by my failed efforts, John barely contains his mirth. I'm furious. "You need to complete the assignment with *that* piece of plaster," John insists. "You can make it into an organic shape but you have to do *something* with it."

Organic shape? Okay, I'll make it organic. Out on the balcony, holding the "thing" over my head, I let it drop. The brick it hits explodes; "it" remains unscathed. The next go is with added force. Same result. Five more tries; nada.

This is how I came to be hanging over the balcony rail watching the "thing" in a three-story freefall; a wild woman yelling, with hair that has taken on an organic shape of its own courtesy of clay and plaster sculpting gel. At last, a slight chip is dislodged. Fetching it, I race back upstairs and hurl it over the side with all my might. Again, a small piece flies off. After a few more times of this anger management exercise, an irregular shape emerges.

John agrees it looks organic. But, I'm not done. He drills a hole in one side so it can be mounted. At the hardware store I find the required screw, locate a piece of wood at my house for the platform, paint the wood black, assemble the two pieces and, *voila!* A study in black and white. *Finis*! Wrong.

Evaluation day. "I can't accept this as a finished piece, Joan," John reports. It's improved but not polished. You need to color it somehow. I'll give you an extension until the last day of class to complete the project."

At home, I sit with that "rock", staring at it; meditating on it. It's hard to let go of the animosity I have developed for this entity. Finally, in some burst of spontaneous combustion seeping through dream work and intuition, I stop at the local craft store, and purchase different bright colors of fabric paint. I can't make it worse. There's nothing to lose. Perhaps that's a good starting place.

The fabric paint is three-dimensional and looking pretty cool. La-de-da-de-da, I'm humming and laughing as I work on it. Finally, I let go completely. I'm over the edge. No expectations. I split here, splat there, rub-a-dub-dub and finally it is complete...or my definition of it, anyway. I'm sure John will want to throw it in the trash. He's not a multi-color psychedelic sort of guy.

On the last day of class when John sees my organic form he starts to laugh with delight! Even his eyes dance! "Joan, did you leave it on a street corner in San Francisco at Mac Arthur Park with the paints beside it? Did everyone who passed by stop and add a bit of their own thing to it?" he asks. John proclaims it's so bad, a mix of Peter Max and acid rock, that it's good! Another student even wants to buy it!

A few weeks later, I'm at the college bookstore and impulsively purchase a copy of Peck's *Sculpture as Experience*. Somewhere, deep in my psyche, a window is slightly opening to sculpture. Hmmmm....a disturbing development indeed.

Riverside Blues

Nothing about smog is fair. The assholes in West LA make most of it but hardly see any of it. The wind blows it inland. The mountains hold it in place. It comes here to live.

I work in LA myself. Most nights, I sleep there, too. But *mi amor,* she lives out here. We're supposed to see each other on the weekends. The weeks keep getting longer.

Sixty five miles is not a great distance. I know this. Just as I know that there are star-crossed lovers strung throughout the corners of the globe, waiting, impatient, lonely, longing, awake at all hours, alternately cursing and praying for the bittersweet consolation of the video call that may never come. We used to be those lovers.

Back here in the land of automotive standards, people say: "It's an hour." We use time as a measurement of distance as if distance had no say of its own. This is a prime example of the boundless optimism for which this land is rightly known. When we say, "it's an hour," we're trying to convince ourselves, as if the saying made it so.

I drove to Riverside once on a Friday after work. It took two and a half hours. You can't do that every day both ways. So, I stay out in LA most nights but *mi amour,* she lives out here.

Hot Fall Thursday Morning

Sitting in the car
On some street I don't know
Watching the garbage truck
Pull up in front of one house
Then the next

The truck has a grabber
That picks up the cans
Whirls them into the air
And turns them upside down
Emptying the contents into the truck

Thanks to this hydraulic grabber
The guy driving the truck
Works all by himself
All day, everyday
One house, then the next

I look at the driver as he passes
He's wearing earplugs
To dampen those same sounds
The whir of the grabber
The trash crashing into the truck

He must hear those same sounds
All day, everyday
But do you even hear
What you hear
All day, everyday

It's a hot Fall Thursday morning
And I couldn't hear nothing
Not the moan of the car
Not the music on the radio
Nothing

And then the garbage truck came
With its brash crashing
Up and down the street
And I hear that and it feels good

Michelle Swims with Gold

Dinner was great, but barbeque chicken is always delicious, you can't go wrong. As we were finishing our coffee, everyone was commenting on how they hated to see the summer coming to a close. It had seemed so short. We should take the kids on a picnic to the river, before they had to go back to school.

"Good," someone said. "How about tomorrow?" Before anyone had a chance to veto the idea, we were discussing what we would need to take, what snacks we would need and who would bring what. It wasn't long and we were filling the car with things that could be loaded early: bathing suits, towels, blankets to sit on, non-perishable snacks.

The next morning, all we had to do was put in the ice chest, sodas, lunch meat, etc. On the way, we stopped and got more drinks, potato salad and ice. Then we were on our way, singing the songs we knew the words to and lots of new ones. The kids were off-key, but we didn't mind, because they were happy and we were having a good time.

When we got to the river, it was so cool, you could almost taste it. We could smell the freshness of it and feel the moisture as it rippled along. There were enough trees hovering over the beach with the sun sneaking through, so the sand wasn't hot, just right.

I found a perfect spot where the trees made a canopy over us, put the blanket down and sat on it. My husband, Lee, brought our 6-month-old baby, Michelle -we called her Missy- out of the car and put her on the blanket next to me.

Missy loved looking up at the movement of the leaves while the wind bounced them around, and the birds chirped as they flew through the branches. Her little cheeks swelled up into a smile and her arms and legs paddled like a turtle turned upside down. Her long eyelashes framed her big brown eyes. She seemed hypnotized by the action taking place above her. The family unpacked the rest of the things from the car and Lee, his sister, her husband and their kids went further downstream where the water was shallow enough for our four-year-old daughter to swim and I could watch them play.

After a while, I realized the coffee was in a pile with beach chairs, fishing poles, the cooler, and the picnic basket, about 12 feet away from me, in the opposite direction from the water. I went over to get it. When I turned around to check on Missy, she was gone from the blanket. I realized that I had been sitting between her and the river. When I got up, she had seen the river and crawled toward it.

As I started running she was crawling into the river and soon all I could see was the bottom of her diaper.

My heart fell into my stomach. I felt like I'd never be able to breathe again. She was gone, the river had taken her.

I felt like I was running in slow motion. I couldn't move any faster, but it suddenly dawned on me that if I kept running toward her, she would keep going further downstream.

I changed my direction, so I could maybe get ahead of her. I tried to shout to my husband, who was standing down river with the others where Missy was heading, but they couldn't hear me. I knew by the time she got there it would be too late anyway, if they saw her at all, she could float right by and they'd never even know it was her. All they would see was just a diaper in the water.

I ran as fast as I could, fearing that when I got in the water, it would slow me down. What could I do to move faster? Could I swim in shallow water? Surely swimming would be faster than running? What if the river took her to the deeper side? I wouldn't be able to swim back with her in enough time to revive her. If that happens, I thought maybe I should try to hold her out of the water until the river takes us to her dad. He's taller than me; he could get to shore faster.

"Oh, please don't let me lose her!" I chanted over and over again.

I must have gotten an extra burst of energy, because I seemed to fly right through the water. Missy and I arrived at the same spot at the same time.

The water never got above my knees and I lifted her up with her face down in case she had water in her mouth; gravity would pull it out before she could swallow it.

To my surprise and relief, she was laughing and kicking. Apparently she was mesmerized looking at the fool's gold along the bottom of the clear river, and had not taken a breath yet.

With big tears in my eyes, I sat down in the shallow water and held her close to my heart. I rocked her in my arms, vowing to never let her leave me again.

School Bus Baby

Sept. was here and school was just starting after a long hot summer. It's early in the morning and everyone is still half asleep. Everybody is bumping into each other, trying to find out where they should be and which way to go. As five school buses in a row pulled up to the curb where we drop off, me and the other drivers are trying to snug up to the bus in front of us, so a kid can't squeeze in between and maybe get hurt. We have to count the little passengers as they get off the bus, but they are pushing each other, tickling, wrestling, and jumping back on, stating they forgot something.

We finally got a chance to take a breath and someone started honking at the car in front of them, trying to enter the circle to drop off their kids. Some cars trying to get in and some cars trying to be on their way, as they weaved in and out of the traffic, trying to miss hitting a kid or bending fenders.

Parents are starting to yell "you forgot your lunch, money, or kisses". Teachers are out trying to control the traffic, hollering "stop running" or "look out for that car". There is a crossing guard at the street hoping no one jumps off the curb.

A mother with a baby in a stroller and a big white shepherd dog was walking her child to school. Before she kissed her daughter goodbye, she tied the dogs leash to the stroller and turned to wave at her as she was leaving. The little girl was waving back.

I put my school bus in gear, checking the rear view mirror, getting ready to merge out into the traffic. The other drivers were doing the same. If all the buses are ready to go, out of courtesy, you allow the buses in front of you to go out first, so we often pull out into traffic in a row, all at one time.

Hardly anyone noticed the cat walking by, but the dog did. He took off after it, dragging the attached stroller with him. He darted out into traffic, crossing the street, causing all the cars to jerk to a stop. All five school buses screeched to a halt, with the brakes squealing. We almost slammed into each other, missing by only inches. Everybody watching was filled with horror. The teachers were covering their mouths and parents were gasping as the stroller went bouncing all over the road, while the dog was trying to run faster. Everybody tried to block the path of the dog or do something.

Finally, someone was able to grab the dog's collar, and by that time, the school nurse was on her way to the stroller. She checked the baby out and took her from her belts. The baby was laughing and smiling, apparently she was having a good time, like on a roller coaster. The nurse said, "Because she was strapped in good, she was unharmed, except for being shook up, she seems to have survived the ride very well".

The Facts of Life

It's 1981 and near the end of summer in Ontario, California, a small low income suburb about 50 miles east of Los Angeles. Our house is the color of dirt. Large bushes stand in front of its two windows that face the street. The yard needs to be mowed. A tattered blue pick-up truck with an equally tattered camper shell sits in the driveway, along with a small brown Pinto station wagon. Loud yells and screams are coming from inside. You can hear glass breaking, a door slamming.

My mother comes storming out of the house, dragging my younger sister Annie by the hand. Annie is 8 years old, two years younger than me and my twin sister Jackie. Annie is crying, fat tears running down her face, her long brown hair disheveled. "I don't want to go by myself," she sobs. My dad walks outside. His white skin is sunburned bright red and his ample stomach bulges out of the bottom of his green Mayflower uniform. "Judy, get back here, don't leave," he pleads. "No, fuck you, John, I'm leaving you! You son of a bitch! Keep those fucking twins, they're little bitches. I'll take Annie", my mom yells back.

Jackie and I are hiding on top of the roof, shivering in the sun in our one piece OP swimsuits. My swimsuit is black with a rainbow stripe down the side. We stare at the chaotic, but familiar scene below. It is almost like a dysfunctional version of the sitcoms we watch so obsessively on TV.

As they drive away, I feel as if I swallowed a grapefruit whole. Would my mom run a red light and get hit by a semi, would she hit the center divider on the freeway and get them pinned and trapped inside the car, or would she never come back?

My mother pushes Annie into the back seat screaming, "Stop fucking crying." As she starts the car, my dad runs to the car and bangs on the window. My mom flips him off and drives away. I see Annie craning her head out the window looking up at the roof; I wave.

My father shakes his head and shouts in the sky, "Girls, where are you?" We slowly scoot down the slanted roof on our behinds and go backwards down the ladder to the ground. My dad comes into the back yard and gives me a hug, which I try and squirm out of. "Let's go get pizza," he says with a smile. His eyes stay sad. Jackie pats his shoulder as we walk inside the house to change.

When we get to the Pizza Hut, my dad orders a medium pepperoni pizza, a pitcher of root beer and a pitcher of Budweiser. He feeds the small black and white TV with a dollar's worth of quarters; each quarter is 15 minutes of TV time. We watch "Different Strokes" then "The Facts of Life". My dad would rather be watching "MASH." We gulp down the root beer as my father downs glass after glass of beer. I put a piece of pizza on his plate, "Hurry and eat, Dad, before Jackie eats it all." Jackie punches my arm. We fight over the last slice of pizza and I finally give in. Jackie stuffs the last piece of pizza in her mouth and says with cheese and sauce dribbling down her chin, "Annie is going to be mad she missed this." I laugh and get up to go to the bathroom. When I am almost done peeing, I flush the toilet and think, "If I can finish before the flushing stops, then they're OK." I finish right before the flushing stops and cross myself.

I walk slowly back to the red and white checkered table and see my sister prodding my father awake, "C'mon, Dad, time to go." His pitcher is empty. My sister and I climb into the back of the shell and lay our heads down on green packing blankets. The truck swerves a bit as we turn down Grove Avenue and I poke my head through the cab to check on him. At the stop light by the baseball park, he starts crying. "Your mom is crazy, one day she is going to kill you guys. I know it, that's why I can't leave."

"It's OK, Dad, she'll be there when we get home, she'll be calm," I say.

Later that night, I sit in my bed reading one of my mother's Harlequin romances; we have a whole library full of them, almost five hundred in all. My dad built some bookshelves in the garage to house them all. I love the way the words express such longing and desire.

Jackie is asleep in the bed next to mine, her blue and white striped K-Mart comforter tucked under her chin. She's drooling onto her pillow. We share a room because Jackie is afraid to sleep alone. Annie has her own room next door which she keeps padlocked so that we won't touch her stuff. My dad built our beds into the wall and placed them vertical to one another and painted them both a chalky white color even though I wanted mine painted mint green. Jackie is scared of the dark, so she prefers to sleep with the lights on. I always turn out the lights as soon as she falls asleep. I make sure that her Wonder Woman night light is plugged in the socket next to her bed.

I can hear my dad snoring. As soon as we got home he passed out on his power blue La-Z-Boy recliner. The chair smells like his sweat. I hear the key turning in the front door and my mom saying, "Wake up John, wake up, it's late". After he mumbles her name, she says, "You smell like beer, go to bed." I hear her help him up and as they pass my bedroom, I hear a thump and my mom saying, "Dammit, John! You almost broke him!"

I think my dad just bumped into the two foot plaster Jesus that sits in the hallway. Even though I know God wouldn't like it, I wish he had broken the statute. Whenever I walk past it in the hallway, his Jesus eyes seem to follow me, as if he is going to reach out his stigmata covered palm and touch me. Sometimes the statute speaks to me in my dreams. I can never remember what he says.

A few minutes later, Annie pads into my room, holding her Baby Fresh Doll and whispers, "Jenny, are you awake?" I lift my head from my prayers and pat the bed beside me. As she blows her hot chocolate tinged breath on me, I breathe a sigh of relief.

Holiday Blues

Growing up, holidays and parties at our house always resulted in chaos. They started out good and ended bad. The better they were, the worse they ended. This is a story of one such day.

My mom wakes us up on Saturday morning at 7 a.m. by yelling, "Get up! People are coming over. Get this pigsty cleaned up!"

The house is a wreck as usual, so we help my mom clean the house all morning. My mom loathes laziness. If we dare complain, she tells us the all too familiar story of her picking strawberries one summer and how it was the hardest summer of her life.

My sisters and I start with the living room. I use the vacuum to get all of Whitey's cat hair off of the couch. My cat Whitey is a long haired Persian with snow white fur and eyes the color of emeralds.

After we finish cleaning the inside of the house, we clean the patio area and the pool. I hoist the pool net's handle over my shoulder and run it through the pool while Jackie and Annie sweep the patio area.

The song "Roseanna" by Toto blasts from the speakers of the boom box plugged in the corner of our backyard. Whenever that song plays, my dad mentions Barbara, because her five year old daughter is named Roseanna. Barbara is my dad's daughter from his first wife, Tiny. Barbara lives in the trailer park behind the bar my parents own. My dad has another daughter from Tiny named Roberta and she lives in South Dakota with her husband, Chuck. When we were five, my twin sister Jackie and I were the flower girls at her wedding. That was six years ago.

The bar my dad owns is called "The Big O". I think it had that name when they bought it. It is right down the street in Ontario located on Holt just east of Grove Avenue. My mom never wanted the bar. She says that a drinker owning a bar is a disaster waiting to happen.

On the weekends, we help my dad clean the bar. We brush down the pool tables while he makes us food from the bar: hot dogs, hamburgers, and frozen pizzas. When dad turns his back to load the beer cooler, Jackie or I slip in behind the cigarette machine and steal a couple packs of Marlboros. We smoke one pack through-out the week and sell the rest at school for a quarter a cigarette. Annie always threatens to tattle, so we pay her off.

Once the leaves are swept up, the pool looks like clean blue sky. The tile on the pool is dark blue with gold specks. My parents put the pool in after we begged them and had to take something called a second on the house. I don't know what a second is, but I love my pool. I am at peace underwater.

Richard and his wife arrive to the pool party at noon along with their two kids. Richard works with my dad at Mayflower, a moving company. My dad used to drive sixteen wheeler trucks long distance, but he gave it up so that he could spend more time at home. Richard is darkly handsome with a thick head of hair.

"He looks like Ponch from CHIPS," I whisper to Jackie.

CHIPS is one of our favorite shows on TV. It comes on at three p.m., and we run home from school everyday and turn on the TV so we don't miss the opening theme song.

A little later, Johnny Rietner and his wife arrive with their kids. We always call Johnny Reitner by his first and last name because he and my dad share the same first name.

"John, how you doing?" Johnny Reitner says and slaps my dad's hand. My dad hands him a beer.

Johnny Reitner has a bright red shock of hair and his white arms are dotted with freckles. My mom hates my dad hanging out with him because she says he is white trash. He looks like Richie Cunningham to me.

I strut around in my new yellow bikini with ties on the side. Jackie is wearing a blue and pink bikini and Annie has on a one piece. Whenever I get mad at Jackie, I call her a cow, but she is only about ten pounds heavier than I am. Jackie and I have short curly hair like my mom and Annie has long straight hair that falls right below her butt.

My sisters and I have an unofficial competition for which one of us can get the darkest, and after we sunbathe for an hour, we pull down our bathing suit straps to compare who has the most dramatic tan.

Later that afternoon, I relax on a blue plastic blow up floater reading one of my mom's Harlequin novels. She has hundreds of them in the bookcases my dad built for her in the garage. My mom always lets me read them when she is finished. I love the way the stories always have romantic, happy endings.

I slather baby oil all over myself until I glisten like a baby seal. The sun warms my brown skin. It feels like the most beautiful day in the world.

As I paddle the floater along the side of the pool, Jackie tries to knock me over. I slap her away and shout, "Stop it. You're being a shit head."

Jackie looks at me. I think I hurt her feelings until she sticks her tongue out and makes a funny face. "Pull me," I say in my bossy oldest twin voice. Jackie obeys and swims as fast as she can as she tugs me along in my floater. We move along the pool's edge and tell stories about a fake world like the one with puppets in Mister Roger's Neighborhood.

"That's the enchanted land," I explain to Jackie, as we pass by the planter with the geraniums in it. "Fairies live in there." Jackie smiles, she loves make believe. Jackie has the best imagination of all of us and pretends her stuffed Pot Belly Bear can talk. Pot Belly is the bear from the Bear Jamboree at Disneyland.

After a while, I get tired of laying on the floater and flip myself over. The water is cool, not cold. I swim the length of the pool underwater and hold my breath the entire time like a mermaid. Later, Johnny Reitner's kids jump off of the diving board one at a time and swim past each other while the other kids laugh and wrestle. I organize a game of Marco Polo with the oldest boys who attend Mariposa Elementary with me. "Marco," I shout with my eyes closed. When I hear a voice say, "Polo", I follow the voice and tag someone.

My dad stands in front of the barbeque in his usual blue swim trunks and a white t shirt. He hates wearing shorts because his legs are swollen from his high blood pressure and job moving furniture. Dad is already sun burnt and on at least his fifth Budweiser.

Annie sneaks up behind him and in one gulp, she downs the rest of the can he has sitting on the picnic table. He catches her with the can tilted above her mouth and swipes at her and says in a laughing voice, "Annie, don't do that."

Johnny Reitner looks at my dad and grins when my dad says, "She loves beer just like her daddy."

I watch as my dad crumples his can and before he asks, I run and hand them both cold Budweisers out of the cooler. "Thanks Jenny, that's my girl," my dad says with a relaxed smile.

My mom walks outside, her arms folded across her chest. Her curly short black hair is pulled back with a brown headband. Her dark skin stands out against her white tank top and white shorts.

It is only three o' clock, but I think she is mad because she has to go to work soon at the restaurant. My dad teases her, trying to get her to laugh. "C'mon Judy, relax," he says in a slurred voice. I can tell his teasing is beginning to get on her nerves.

Johnny Reitner's wife turns to my mom with a smile. "How's work, Judy?"

Everyone knows my mom is a waitress at Yanghtzee, a Chinese restaurant in town. My mom's smile is a bit forced as she shrugs and says, "Same old, same old. Edna won't buy us anything for the restaurant and Robin wants every weekend off, including today, so I have to go to work at five."

Johnny Reitner walks around to face her and puts his arm around her shoulders and says, "C'mon, Judy, have a good time. Relax and have a beer."

"Uh oh," I thought to myself. I knew my mom wouldn't like that comment.

My mom looks at him and wiggles out of his grasp with an exasperated look and says, "OK, Johnny, should I drink a twelve pack and drive to work?"

My dad and Johnny Reitner crack up, drunk with more than laughter. My mom turns away with a grunt.

I watch as my dad places huge steaks on the grill four at a time. Smoke rises from the glowing embers.

"C'mon girls, time to eat," he yells when the steaks are done. Jackie and I fight each other for the front of the line and as we walk up my dad puts a steak on each of our paper plates. "Put some of that Worcestershire sauce on there," he says handing me the bottle, and I sprinkle it on top of the steak. "And get some of my famous mustard potato salad," he adds. "I made one without onions for Annie."

My mom stands by the screen door and glares at him.

"Mom, come and eat," I say. She walks over slowly to make herself a plate. She swipes my dad's hand away as he pulls at her shorts.

"Stop it, John, I want to eat. I gotta go to work soon," she says in a short voice.

My dad bulges his eyes out, which makes her laugh. He pulls her down next to him on the picnic table.

The fatty sides of my rib eye steak poke off the edges of my plate. My sisters and I sit together on the far end of the picnic table and shovel spoonful after spoonful of potato salad into our mouths. We guzzle can after can of grape Shasta cola. After we finish eating, I burp. Jackie follows my burp with a louder burp of her own. Annie grimaces and hands us napkins when we wipe our faces with our hands. Even though Annie is two years younger than us, she makes us mind our manners.

I turn to find that my mom and dad are not at the table anymore. I see them fighting through the glass patio door. Mom yells at dad, "You're drunk, John. You're a god damn filthy drunk." I can almost feel it coming. My stomach hurts and I can feel the steak sitting in the pit of my stomach like a dead weight.

A few minutes later, my mom emerges from the house with her crazy "don't mess with me" look in her eyes.

"It's time for you to go," she says to everyone. No one pays her any attention, everyone is eating. "Time to go," she shrieks and screams in a

126

loud banshee voice, "Get the fuck out!" Everyone turns to look at my mom. It turns quiet.

"Cuckoo cuckoo," Jackie says in my ear. I nudge her quiet.

Johnny Reitner's wife shakes her head as they pack up their stuff and walk out the back fence without a word. Richard and his wife glance at us with a worried look as they leave with kids in tow.

"Shit, here it goes again," Jackie says softly. I nod my head. Annie shakes in her swimsuit like a scared little rabbit and I grab her towel and put it around her shoulders.

My parents go inside. I can hear them screaming and yelling at one another in the house and throwing things. A tear rolls down Annie's face and I put my arm around her and Jackie grabs her hand.

The window to my parent's bedroom looks out onto the pool and we all place our faces against the glass and watch my mom beat on my dad with her fists. Dad turns around and pushes my mom into the wall head first.

Jackie, Annie and I gather around the picnic table. "Should we go? Jackie asks. "Just wait," I say. Jackie and Annie sit down by the pool with their feet in the water.

It doesn't stop. My dad runs out of the back door with my mom right after him. She throws a plate at him and shards of glass litter the patio floor. "Get the fuck out of here, John," she screams as she clutches her face. Her eye looks swollen.

I hear my dad's pickup truck revving up and then more screaming and fighting as he pulls away. Minutes later, my mom races back into the backyard from the side gate and screams, "Get out of here, girls."

She does not need to tell us twice.

Annie runs out the back gate first and streaks down the street in her towel and swimsuit. Jackie races to catch her and I follow behind. I had to make sure and grab my book.

John Glenn Park is right around the corner. A slightly rusted swing set sits on dried out grass along with a monkey bar set and a large circular maze that looks like a big piece of orange cheese. I go to my usual place inside the plastic cheese. I like its twisting holed walls even though it smells like pee.

Jackie pushes Annie on the swing. Her hair trails behind like a fan. The higher Jackie pushes her, the more Annie giggles. I wonder if everyone's life is like this. Jackie waves her hand at me, a sign she wants me to come over so I wipe my face and close my Harlequin book.

My head is swimming as if I am still underwater. I walk out to the swings and wince when I see my mom's brown Pinto drive by. I watch as my mom turns her head to look at us. I hope she drives away, but instead she motions for us to come over. We walk over and when we get closer she yells, "I am going to go find your father. Go home."

We stay at the park. I watch the sun set from inside my plastic cheese and wonder why good days always had to go bad.

I wish I was someone else, anyone, but me.

Hours later, I hear my mom's voice echoing over the street to the park, "Girls, come back. Please come back." The three of us take our time walking back home.

Daisies Through the Concrete

Jesus Christ, Hazel thought to herself as she was waiting for the number 3 bus that would take her to get her sonogram, *it's been three months and they still can't tell me what the hell's wrong with me.* The doctors threw around words like *cancer, celiac disease, diabetes,* and other terms that just kept getting scarier. The pain in her abdomen was such a constant thing now that she just learned to live with it, but tried not to make it worse. It made her afraid to eat, so much so that she lost twenty-five pounds in a little over a month and had to force herself to eat—even if it was nothing more than a banana and saltines with a multi-vitamin.

She instinctively touched the black and blue bandana wrapped around her head like a headband that kept her unruly black hair out of her face. It was a gift from her grandmother, handed down from generations to women who were born keepers of the magic, and one of the only things she had to hand down to Hazel before she died. She learned about magic from her Grandma Morgan, who came to America from Ireland in the fifties with little else but her name and her stories, and left the land of the living very much in the same fashion. It was her grandmother's stories and lessons that were keeping Hazel together these days.

Hazel sighed heavily, trying to expel her worries with her breath. She tried not to think about the things that threatened to pull her down, even though she was conscious of the fact that she was barely keeping her head above water. She tried not to think about the rejection letters from the scholarship committees. She certainly didn't want to think about looking at her phone and the missed call log full of "no number"—most likely from the creditors she was trying to appease and failing miserably. It was enough to want to make her angst, anger, and feelings of helplessness and futility come with a body count consisting of those assholes who worked for the card companies and the scholarship committees, and her parents, who sold what little was left of Grandma Morgan's possessions to get her brothers out of jail and into rehab, knowing full well that they were fuck ups with no intention of becoming sober and also knowing that Hazel, despite having two jobs, still needed help with tuition and bills. She often wondered that with all the crap that people go through, that they only use ten percent of their brains.

She wished in the worst way that her grandmother was with her.

Hazel's grandmother made the world make sense for her. She would have taught her something that would make all her problems seem miniscule—hell, she'd make her see it so it was funny. She taught Hazel about magic, but now she couldn't see it, and she couldn't seem to find it anywhere. She felt like she had none left. She remembered a story her grandmother told her, about how a group of scared and ignorant villagers that killed the unicorn that helped purify their well so the town's children wouldn't get sick anymore. That unicorn was the last unicorn, and when it died, all the light and magic in the world died with it. "But you have to find your own magic, be your own fairy godmother. Make your magic and look for it in everything, Punky" Hazel's grandmother told her after she finished the story.

Hazel tried not to cry, as she was in public in broad daylight in the middle of San Bernardino. The city was like an old pomegranate, dried up and rotting from the inside out, with old buildings that had yet to be torn down, and people hardened by crime and poverty. The only reason she lived there was to go to school. She hardly left campus, only taking buses to get to work, the grocery store or the bank—when she had enough money for food or money to deposit in the bank. Hazel hated the city, but she appreciated its grittiness and knew herself well enough to know she could handle it.

The sun had hardly been up in the sky very long. It was still waking up and climbing slowly upwards. The temperature was climbing, as well, and Hazel knew to find shade, as she had a long day outdoors in front of her and did not want to let her pale skin burn. Hazel looked at sun, not caring if she went blind, much like the Sioux women she read about, who once a year would participate in what seemed like masochistic rituals where the men would pierce their backs and hang buffalo skulls, or pierce their chests and hang from a pole. Maybe they thought through their pain, they could gain some deep spiritual insight or great power. *If whatever doesn't kill you makes you stronger, we'd all be gods by now.*

"Excuse me, Miss?" a voice intruded into her thoughts. Hazel quickly turned her head to the voice and found a man in front of her. He was wearing black trousers that were stained, a red shirt, a black tweed sport coat, and a sharp looking black fedora. His dark face was glowing from the sun, and his teeth shined through his full lips. His small dreads had wiry threads of gray, as did his goatee. His black eyes and his glasses reflected the sun, but it looked to Hazel that the orange dot in each pupil emanated from within. Despite his secondhand mish mashed clothes, he sported an impeccably clean and new looking black leather satchel. Hazel didn't know what to do or to make of him, so she just raised her eyebrows and tilted her head.

130

"Sorry, Miss, but do you have a light?" He asked in a voice that was as cool and smooth as a milkshake.

"I'm sorry, I don't," she answered quietly. The stranger found a light from another man walking down the street, but didn't drag on his cigarette.

"What's your name, Sweetheart?" the stranger asked her.

Wonderful, a pimp with a profit margin. She knew to be careful in Berdu and around strangers. "Ray," she lied.

"Well, Ray, my name is Z."

"Z?"

"Z Artist, at your service," he replied and tipped his hat. "I was wondering if you'd be so kind as to let me draw you. You're inspiring me right now, and I have to draw you."

Hazel didn't know what to think, but saw no immediate harm. "Um, okay."

Just as she gave her permission, Z had a pen and a sketchpad ready. He handed Hazel a small red leather book. "That's a portfolio of my work," he explained, "I've had the pleasure of working in New Orleans, San Francisco, New York, Oakland, and right here in the city of Saint Bernard." Hazel leafed through the book and found shop signs and realistic looking portraits in both black and white and color. At the end of the book, she found a couple of pictures that looked like they were taken in the late seventies or early eighties, judging by the woman in the picture's clothes and beaded cornrows. She was playing what looked like a Gibson Les Paul in a deep cherry color that complimented her chocolate kiss skin. She was beautiful, her face reminded Hazel of Nefertiti and Grace Jones, with high cheekbones, equine nose, and full, bee stung lips.

"Ah, now that lady is a special one," Z commented. "I met her in New York when I was a young man. She was the only black woman I knew who could play guitar as well as Jimi Hendrix, and left handed, too. I was in love with her, but for some reason, I knew it was better to stay friends with a precious pearl of a woman like that. I haven't seen her in fifteen years, but I still think about her to this day, and I hope that wherever she is, that's she's happy and safe." Z's cigarette, which he never smoked, burned down to the filter, so Z dropped it onto the sidewalk. He was drawing the whole time he was talking, making long, fast strokes with his pen. "Your hair is wild, and I'm trying to get it just so," he commented, "it's like you're a wild jungle girl who was raised by wolves. Do you know about wolves, Ray?"

"A little bit." Hazel noticed that some people were staring, but she didn't care. As Z talked, time seemed to slow to an almost standstill and the derelict shops and people were melding together in an impressionistic swirl painting.

Z smiled. "Wolves, in many a Native American thought, are the great teacher. They are the best example of how people should live: they only kill to eat, they're monogamous, and they love and protect their young. Each one in a pack knows their place, and though their place may change, they make the best of the position they're in. You remind me of a wolf, with your features, Ray. I can see in your kaleidoscope eyes a deep, instinctual wisdom. Are you Native American, perchance?"

"I don't think so," she replied.

"What about Irish?"

"My grandmother emigrated here from there," she answered before she could stop herself.

"That explains it, then." Z replied.

"Explains what?" Hazel inquired.

The two looked at each other: Z trying to probe Hazel, and Hazel trying not to let him in. Z simply smiled and looked down at his sketch pad. "The ancient Celts and the Native Americans have a lot in common in that they have a respect for the earth and an understanding of magic that can only be described as intuitive. I see that knowledge in you. Your eyes are like murky lakes in that one doesn't know how deep they go, and I also see a wisdom that betrays your age; you look in your early twenties, but you may as well be two-hundred." He never looked up from his sketch pad as he spoke. Hazel was speechless and tried to hide it; he could tell that to anybody and they would think he was psychic.

"I bet you say that to everyone," Hazel commented cynically.

"I see, Ray, what you mean. This city's a bad mother if you're not careful. You're hip to the jive, and I see that along with your pepper spray. I don't claim to be a psychic. I just call 'em like I see 'em."

Hazel felt bad for doubting Z. The man meant no harm. Sure, he was eccentric, but not dangerous. "So, Z, what do you know about magic?" she asked him.

"Not much, Ray, but I know that in this day and age, there are people who fight to make their own magic, even when it seems that there's none left in the world. I know that you most likely feel that you're lost and you can't find your own anymore, especially since it seems that the odds aren't in your favor. But I know, Miss Ray, that if you change the way you're thinking, your loser's luck will turn. I also know that if you live in the present, you won't have that frown on your face anymore. I'm pretty sure your grandmother taught you all this, but you somehow forgot it and need to be reminded of it."

Hazel knew Z was right. Grandma Morgan taught her to live in the present, to not fret on the past and not worry about the future. "What's said and done is said and done, Punky," Hazel heard Grandma say, "and the future may not get here, so all you can do is live *now*. Believe me, right now there's nothing wrong: You're alive and there's no immediate threat, so get on with it!" Hazel smirked in spite of herself.

"Aha! Done!" Z exclaimed, "But you know what, Ray? This is too good and I'm afraid I'm gonna have to keep it, but lemme conjure up something else for you to thank you for your inspiration." Z sketched furiously for a minute and ripped the paper out of the pad. "Here you are."

Hazel looked at the sketch and saw an angel playing a guitar. The angel had wild hair and a halo and sharp wings. The feminine figure and face were drawn with minimal lines and the whole thing was beautiful in a minimalist way. Hazel was touched and amazed at Z's talent. "Thank you," she gushed as she fished in her pocket for a couple of bills to hand to Z.

"No need, Ray, as I said, that's my thank you for inspiring me," he smiled as he explained. The number 3 was rolling in. "Again, thank you. And keep on keeping on. Things will get better for you, I know it." Z took Hazel's hand and kissed it gently before walking away. Hazel blushed and tilted her head to the ground, where she found a daisy through a crack in the concrete. She picked it up and put it in her hair just as the bus stopped in front of him.

Firebreather

Fun fact: as a comedian, I'm contractually obligated to talk shit about the place I'm in. I'm also contractually obligated to make you clap one more time for all the acts that came before me, but since I'm the first one on, I guess we can forego that.

Anyway, I think my favorite thing about the Inland Empire is the name. I mean, who came up with that? I know it had something to do with real estate wanting the area to sound more appealing to outsiders, but c'mon. They tried switching the name of Wineville to Mira Loma but that doesn't change the fact that all those chicken murders happened there and now Clint Eastwood has another million bucks in the bank! He even put the word "change" in the movie title and it didn't help. And what the hell makes this place an "empire," anyway? I'm half-expecting to see soldiers with Marvin the Martian hats walking around every damn corner I turn. *imitating Marvin the Martian* We're about to invade Orange County. Isn't that lovely?

Honestly, that's something I would love to see.

I keep seeing this vanity plate on campus that reads O-C-N-8-I-V. Get it? OC native? If you're so damn proud of being from Orange County then why the fuck did you end up here? And that's the only thing I've seen like that! What is it about Orange County-ites that's make them wanna announce to the world where they're from? It's not like I have an "Idaho represent!" sticker on my car, or anything. People, this brings me to my favorite word in the French language: DOUCHE!

They meet at a black box performance venue on campus, right after he's done with a show. He's still sweating from the lights, epinephrine fresh in his system, hoping one day he'll get paid to do this, which is basically complain in front of an audience for an hour and a half. He buys her a cherry daiquiri and that night they make love, violating the rules of the dorm and even going so far as to betray the Resident Manager's trust, who lives in the same apartment as her. She doesn't seem at all worried about getting caught. She's as confident as he is. The next day, he escapes to an early theater class where he asks his classmates questions like, "If Stu chews shoes, should Stu choose the shoes he chews?"

And they date. And the relationship flourishes. And one month later, he does another show, his new girlfriend in the standing room, right in front, him wondering to the audience why "asshole" is one of the words you can't say on TV. "What if you flip-flopped the words? Asshole! BLEEP! Hole ass? No bleep!

"And speaking of whole asses, back when I still lived in Boise, some buddies of mine used to drive into town saying they were looking for a piece of ass. Just a piece! They'd be like, 'You wanna come with? We're looking for a piece of ass!' And I'd say, 'What do you want a piece of ass for? I want the whole ass!'"

And he watches her laugh, because he knows she's his. "I play for keeps, too," she tells him that night, as they violate the building's rules for the umpteenth time, this particular occasion with the Resident Manager completely aware. She doesn't even try to hide her ecstasy.

And the first indication he gets that there might be something "weird" about her family, and more specifically, the city he finds himself attending college in, all relates to the mentioning of two innocent words: "December 88."

"When?"

"When, what?"

"I thought I heard you say a date, or something."

"No, no. I'm talking about Dez."

"A person?"

"Yes."

"Named December 88?"

"Well, we don't really know her name. We just know her by the month and year she took over."

"Took over?"

"The groves. She controls South Rio Seco. She was *sixteen* when she took over. That same year, one of the men she ousted threatened to kill her. Later that day, sitting in church, right there in the pew, the guy who threatened her? His head spontaneously flapped backward like a Muppet, all his blood spraying all over the bibles and hymn books and liturgical calendars. The priest was the only one who saw it happen. Home boy says no one ever touched him. No one slashed him with a knife. There wasn't even anyone sitting nearby who could have done it. The guy's neck just split open, inexplicably. Well, of course there's an explanation. December 88."

His reaction? A laugh. Nothing more. Must be just an urban legend.

When, some months later, she sits up suddenly in bed, the sun still hidden beneath the rim of the horizon, her forehead dripping with sweat and her breath labored and irregular, he remembers a friend joking about how in movies and TV shows whenever someone has a nightmare, they bolt upright, screaming.

"Try it," his friend had suggested.

135

Lillie tries it.

"Agh!"

Nick shakes, suddenly being wrenched from a dream he can't recall. Lillie sits up in bed, eyes wide, hair disheveled, sports bra expanding and contracting with the rapidity of her breath.

"What's wrong?"

"Something happened."

She turns on the light. A cell phone rings.

"Hello?"

She stands, eyes still wide. "A heart attack?" Nodding, as if the person she's talking to can tell she's nodding, she says, "We're on our way."

"We who?" Now Nick pulls his body out of bed, turns left and right in search of a wayward pair of boxer-briefs.

"My Uncle Hank died." One of her arms is through a t-shirt sleeve. The other struggles with her pants zipper.

"I didn't know you had an Uncle Hank."

"No, Nick. You don't understand," she says, her head only halfway inside her shirt. "I need you to come with me."

"I didn't know him."

"Please? For me? You're not supposed to be in my dorm, anyway. We could both be put on probation."

"That never stopped us before."

"Uncle Hank was never dead before."

And if the death of a loved one doesn't concern him, that last statement does. Why should breaking the "overnight guest" rule of the building have anything to do with her Uncle Hank?

The ride over is mostly a blur, Nick struggling to stay awake as street lights and traffic signals wash over the windshield. His eyes start to open again when they briefly pass through the fabled orange groves, "Kept alive by Dez and her perspicacity," she notes, an odd sort of calm having settled in.

"Are you okay?"

She looks at him and nods vigorously, barely paying attention as she turns on a street christened, "Overview Parkway." Briefly, he wonders if it was meant to be called "Overvalued Parkway." Real estate in California, as he understands it, requires one to use their firstborn child as a down payment, and this neighborhood is ridiculous. The houses are gigantic. Dry-level mansions, like someone stole Hollywood Hills and hid it in Rio Seco.

And it gets better. She swings her car into the driveway of a garish remote-control gated entryway, each metal bar topped with a Corinthian-style capital holding a sign proudly announcing, "Phoenix Heights." Lillie stops at a metal box with a payphone-esque keypad and a black-and-cabbage LCD screen scrolling instructions on how to get in. "Um, close your eyes," Lillie says.

Nick sighs and turns his head toward the passenger window, now realizing that he must be looking east because the sun pokes its first morning rays above the hills. "Okay," Lillie says, amidst a buzzing sound emanating from the terminal. The gate opens and in they drive.

The house is at the very end of the cul-de-sac—an obvious custom built, and Nick wonders if they managed to exhume the corpse of Frank Lloyd Wright for the design. The houses they passed along the way were just as prodigious. One was clearly modeled after a medieval castle, complete with (and there's no way Nick can think of this without laughing out loud) big, giant, stone knockers on the front doors.

"What's so funny?" She has the expression of a proper English lady right before uttering the phrase, "We are not amused."

"Oh, nothing," he answers, a poorly stifled snort shooting mucus out his nose.

"There aren't enough cars," Lillie notes as she parks. "Who's missing?"

"They just haven't gotten here yet."

Her uncle's house (at least he assumes it's her uncle's house) is three stories tall with the second floor cantilevered outward, swelling towards the front yard with no beam or load-bearing support column, only the heavy material of the third floor holds it in place, almost like a diving board. There doesn't seem to be much of a color scheme, just white, white and more white, including the bricks and stucco. There's no lawn, only a stretch of gravel (is it quartz?) extending from the sidewalk to the house, several priapismic palm trees rising up, appearing as giant torches.

Inside the house are some of the family members she's never admitted having, and only two he recognizes: her mom and dad, seated on a couch, a box of tissues snug between them. Various men in suits hustle about, plus a few more are still in pajamas. A Hispanic woman in an apron sits on a hearth wiping away tears, and although she's obviously a maid, it's an odd sight for Nick to see hired help weeping along with the family. All around, he can hear the low ambience of numerous voices conversing lightly, with a definite atmosphere of instability—so much so that Nick briefly thinks he's wandered onto the set of *Cherry Orchard*, and certainly not one that takes to the farcical side of the production.

After he takes in the sight of the people cluttered inside, he now has a chance to fully appreciate the size of the house. On the drive up, they had passed a few homes that could fit completely in the living room, and unless his eyes deceive him, through a doorway in the back is what appears to be another living room. He decides the decorator must have had that extremely rare type of color-blindness of not being able to discern any color at all. Upon the white marble floor is a white and black zebra-print rug. The walls are a light cream coloration (but white enough to fit with the theme) and the drapes are a white linen patterned with black art deco trim. Aside from that, all the furniture is of a modern, clean-cut polymer—white, of course—including the casing of a television, at least 60 inches in size. The entire building, it seems, is meant to look like you've just stepped inside an iPod.

I've been dating this girl a month and I don't know a damn thing about her. The realization is jarring. He had only ever visited her parents' place, a suburban home in the hills on the east side—definitely an expensive property, but nothing that suggested to him any wealth beyond your standard middle class family. He decides he's had enough of the taste of his fingernails, and realizes that he's pulling them out of his mouth for the first time that morning. *Is that my heart or is my mutant alien child trying to burst out of my chest?*

"Has this ever happened to you before?" Lillie asks. "A death in the family, I mean."

"A grandparent, but it was one of those situations where they're not suffering anymore, so it was more a relief than anything." He hesitates. "Um, why? This ever happen to you?"

"Not anything this big."

He begins reaching his arms out, making a move to give her a hug, but stops when he notices a man in a cashmere sweater approaching.

"Lillie!"

Lillie introduces him as "Eli the Grape," although judging by the way his skin hangs in folds from the bones of his face, he may as well be called "Eli the Prune."

"Your uncle's upstairs. It happened in his sleep."

"I still can't believe this." She starts up the stairway, Eli following close behind, then stops, turns to Nick, and beckons to follow.

"Did it wake you up, too?" she asks, causing thought lines to form on Nick's forehead as he lifts his feet onto the first step.

"Yeah, it did. Your Uncle Arty has a bruise on his chest the size of a grapefruit. Knocked him right in the ticker, apparently."

"Think DD was trying to get them both?"

"Whoa, whoa, whoa." Nick stops, his ascent to the second story only half complete. "How the hell can someone's death put a bruise on a guy's chest?"

Eli grins, but only with the left corner of his face. For a second, Nick wonders if maybe he's had a stroke in his past. "This is your boyfriend, you say?" he asks Lillie.

"Yeah."

"There's a lot he don't know, huh?"

"Isn't it usually better that way?" She asks her question to Eli, but faces her head at Nick, adding simply, "I told you this was big." Then back to Eli, now continuing the climb: "And *where is* Uncle Arty, anyway? He should be here performing the sending ritual."

Sending ritual?

"Your Uncle Arty took the gang to neutral ground."

Lillie stops dead, just outside a set of doors leading to what Nick assumes to be the master suite. "Where? A cemetery?"

Eli nods his head yes.

"Eucalyptus?"

Eli shakes his head no.

"Oh, shit. Not Evenfall."

"'Fraid so. DD must've felt Hank's death, too. Seems he came down from the mountain. Arty saw it as an act of war, so he went to negotiate with the cold bastard." Lillie stands there, stricken as though she's suddenly been made aware of her own mortality for the very first time. And hell, for all Nick knows, that just might be the case. This mountain Eli refers to must be Mt. Montdragon, a pitiful pile of rocks and dust that Nick thought, upon first seeing it, must have been built by God if God a were a child playing in a sandbox, scooping two mounds of dirt together, topping it with a white cross, and then being called in for supper only to forget his creation forever. In fact, sometimes it seems like that's true for the entire Inland Empire. As for this "DD" person, Nick can only guess who that might be.

"DD," Lillie exhales, wiping a tear from her face. "I saw it as an act of war when he crossed the river."

"Santa Ana doesn't take sides."

Nick asks, "How can a river take sides?"

"That's my point," Eli answers. "She doesn't. Although in the winter of '69 the violence got so bad, she took out both bridges just to keep the blood out of her water."

Nick takes a breath to raise another objection, but never finishes. Instead, Lillie shoves past him to the room across the hall. Eli turns to Nick.

"That means you're up, boyfriend. You're about to meet Blind Simon."

139

Nick doesn't like the butterfly that just found its way into his innards. "Is Def Leopard in there, too?"

"Don't joke. Blind Simon don't like strangers. Can I ask what you do?"

"I'm a student."

"No job?"

"I'm a theater major, so I perform almost nightly. When I'm not doing that, I try my hand at comedy."

"You mean standup? Where at?"

"I can't remember what it's called. It's that place at UCRS that looks like a barn?"

"Isn't it just called the Barn?"

"Is it? Oh. Well, that's one mystery solved."

Eli gives Nick a punch to the shoulder blade. Not a slap, a punch. "Don't worry. This shouldn't be too painful."

Not as painful as a slug to the back, I hope.

They enter. It's the master bedroom, and probably has more square footage by itself than Nick's entire dorm, which he shares with three other boys. The white-bleeding-white look of the house isn't present here. Instead, the walls are an ugly mustard orange, and covered floor to ceiling with family photos. A chandelier hangs from above, one wall is covered by a curtain that might also greenlight as a heavy quilted blanket, and judging by the lines of light shining through its folds, it must also be obscuring a glass door leading to a balcony (overhanging the front yard, Nick guesses). The only decoration in the room not depicting some past memory is a wide painting of a dirt arena where a gold-clad matador swings a cape over a charging bull. Just below that, tangled up in the blankets of a four-post bed, is a pudgy man, balding, purple-faced, and wearing a permanent scowl (and little else). Hair spreads across his chest interrupted by more than a few scars, none of which seem like they're surgical to Nick, but then, what does he know about surgical incisions? The most prominent scar is a red keloid closing the gap between the man's nipples as though a child had played connect-the-dots with a straight razor. Nick steps forward, not quite noticing the other men in the room, and gets a closer look at the dead man's face. His expression drops.

Oh, shit. Uncle Hank. That's what Lillie calls him. But he's seen the man's picture in the paper. He's heard about him via gossip around school. Only nobody's ever called him *Hank.*

"Figured it out, did you?" asks a voice that sounds like it belongs to someone who regularly scrapes his throat with a metal file. Nick turns to find a man bound to a wheelchair due to an almost complete lack of limbs. Both legs are cut off at the knee, the right arm ends in a rounded stump, and the left, well, that's the one that seems to be uninjured. His nose is abnormally large, his face has more ripples than the Sahara desert, and his eyes are covered by thick, Coke-bottle glasses that make Nick wonder how small they'd be if not so comically magnified. "Blind Simon," the man says, offering his stump as though he can shake it (and, biting his lip, Nick accepts the offer).

"Blind Simon, or *Legally* Blind Simon?"

Simon ignores the jape and uses his good hand to work the controls of his wheelchair, maneuvering closer to Nick.

"Who are you?"

"Nick Zavislack. I'm Lillie's boyfriend."

"Zavizlack? What kind of a name is Zavislack?"

"I believe it would be a last name."

Simon turns his head to some of the other men in the room. *They almost look like Secret Service agents.* "Has anybody heard the wise guy over here? I guess he doesn't quite get the picture that Henry Tamberelli is *dead!*" He returns to Nick. "The crappier the joke the bigger the balls, is that it? Or are you just stupid?"

Eli takes a step forward. "This is Lillie's *boyfriend,* Simon. You know what that means."

"Yeah. It means Lillie's dating some guy named Nick Zavislack. And I thought Glenda was nuts when she married a man named Rufsvold." Nick is happy he doesn't say what he's thinking about Blind Simon's name, although there's some comfort in knowing he can still maintain a sense humor despite just having learned he's dating the niece of a mafia don.

"So Arty and del Carmen are having a chat and we're left to sit here and babysit some—"

The door opens. Simon falls silent, along with the rest of the room. Lillie has entered, and behind her is yet another unsavory-looking person sauntering through. This one is a woman, age indiscernible (other than the fact that she's simply "old"), long white hair, pants pulled up to her ribcage, and a gemstone hanging around her neck. It seems to change color, flashing blue to dark, dark to white, white to blue as she shifts her weight, shuffling her feet underneath the low light of the chandelier. "Sibyl!" Simon shouts, but she ignores him, creeping to the body, examining first the dead Uncle Hank, and then the very much alive boyfriend Nick. Her eyes bite like snakes. They're violet—they can't be violet, they must be contacts—and set against the pale skin of her face, they seem to be two shining flames against the cold of winter. "This is him?" she asks, with Lillie nodding behind her. There's no way Sibyl can see her nod, but somehow she understands. The moment she asks, Nick begins backing away slowly. Maybe he can make it through the door without anyone noticing.

"What the hell is the fucking *beldame* doing here?" Eli asks, folding his arms across his chest.

"Ask that again," she replies in a high, squeaky voice, never failing to turn her gaze away from Nick, *"Nicely."*

Does she mean me? "Um," Nick answers, now realizing that his bid for freedom has been crushed. "What are you doing here?"

"For your information, I was asked—no, *demanded* here. I owe a certain someone a favor." Sybil nods at Lillie.

Simon is the only one in the room who doesn't appear intimidated. "What the hell did you do that would put you in a situation to owe a favor to Lillie Rufsvold?"

"Let me just say this," Sybil answers, still fixed in a staring contest with Nick. "You can sense the flame of a person, but not the blood. How was I to know that *Rufsvold* was related to *Tamberelli?"*

Stole the words right out of my mouth, Nick thinks.

"I need everyone but you gone." He points at his chest. "Yes, you," she answers, although she's already begun rifling through a handbag Nick never knew she was holding, and thus, she can't see that he's gesturing. Everyone else in the room balks, Blind Simon in particular. A quick mechanical noise emits from his wheelchair, as though making a move to leave but now thinking different of it. "Go. Now," Sybil commands.

"Why him?" Simon finally asks.

"Because I need a fire close to his." She points at Uncle Hank. "And Lillie's grieving." Everyone else in the room begins queuing up at the exit, Lillie first. Her eyes still whine as she meanders out of the room causing Nick to be overwhelmed with the urge to wipe her tears and tell her everything is going to be okay. Eli is the last to leave, wheeling Simon out the door. "I hope you know what you're doing, Syb."

"I'm older than shine-top, over here." She points at Uncle Hank's bald head. "You think I'm playing games? If I wasn't bound by the oaths that give me my power, I would *never* come to this neighborhood, no matter what you paid me."

Eli pushes Simon out the door and closes it behind him. It's just her and Nick. And the corpse. Sybil still rummages, and for half a second, it seems like her hand reaches deeper into her bag than physically possible.

"How are you feeling," she asks now that everyone is gone. "And don't say, 'Fine.' Nobody's ever fine when someone asks."

"I think my heart dropped somewhere in the vicinity of my left testi-
cle. Which hangs down a little lower than the right. Um, TMI," he adds
when he sees the look on her face.

"I will never understand your generation."

"Can I ask you a question?"

"Yes," Sybil replies. "Of course, whether or not you get an answer
depends on the question."

She looks up at him with her violet eyes, and he decides he now
knows what it's like to be an ant under the focused light of a magnifying
glass. *Did it just get warmer in here?*

"Well, what's your question?"

"Uh, how am I supposed to feel about all of this?"

She thinks for a moment. "You a Scorpio?"

"Yeah. So?"

"Lillie says you're good in bed." Sybil reaches her arm in her hand-
bag and pulls out a large glass bottle filled with a clear liquid. She sets it
aside, and continues her rummaging.

"I don't know how it's any of your business."

"You got fire, boy, and I need lots of it. His fire would be best,"
Once again, she refers to the body. "But it got put out, and his closest
living relatives are either too teary-eyed to give me a good flame, or too
pig-headed to be anywhere else in the Empire other than here, where he
belongs. Honestly, why is Arthur bothering to parlay with that psycho-
path? Back when Old Man Tamberelli was still in charge, he'd just send
the Grape and his killers across the water to crush them into grapejuice.
But don't go soft on me, and don't think you're supposed to *feel* any
which way. Just be your fiery self and maybe I can pull this off."

She pulls another glass bottle out of her bag, this one is smaller, but
she uncorks it and he immediately smells black licorice. Her rummaging
continues.

"But then again," she continues, "I'm not supposed to get involved
unless Dez asks me to, which she never does. I live in her ward," she
adds, as if that's supposed to clarify anything.

She removes a tall drinking glass and sets it on the night stand with
the other items she's picked from her purse.

"Ask me about the bottles."

"What?"

"I didn't say, 'Ask me what.' I said, 'Ask me about the bottles!'"

"Um, what's with the bottles?"

"Spirits!" she exclaims, smiling for the first time that morning. "You
and Lillie share a flame, but not blood. I need something to give you a
boost."

"Um, thank you for clarifying that."

Now she removes a third bottle, this one brown, along with a bag of Hershey's Kisses. "Vodka," she announces pouring a generous helping of the large bottle into the drinking glass, "Oil of anise," she drops just a touch into the vodka, "and caffeine." She uncorks the third bottle and sprinkles in the tiniest amount, so little Nick can barely see any. He wonders for a moment if it's even legal to carry concentrated caffeine in a purse, knowing whatever amount is still in the bottle is likely enough to kill. Finally, she drops in a Hershey's Kiss, stirs the mixture with her finger, and hands it to Nick, not hesitating to stick her wet digit in her mouth and close her eyes as though breaking for a quick visit to heaven.

Nick holds the glass gingerly, watching the ripples of the liquid slosh ever so slightly in his shaking hands. "And this helps how?"

"Drink up!" she commands, but when the liquid reaches his throat he coughs and gags and feels the hot substance smoldering back up into his nostrils.

"It burns," he complains, almost spilling the glass with another violent cough.

"What'd you expect? I'm giving you fucking alcohol!"

"I don't normally drink."

She rolls her eyes. "In my day, when grown-ups said, 'Kids these days,' it was because they were getting into trouble, not staying out of it! Just hurry up and finish it. You ever hear the expression 'tear the Band-Aid off?'"

Nick nods, and nearly chokes on the glass as he forces it into his mouth. Immediately, he's reminded how Caesar's wife in the Shakespearian play of the same name killed herself by swallowing hot coals. He reckons this must be how it felt like. Honestly, how the hell could anyone do this so much it becomes a habit?

"Done?" she asks. He nods, his face turning bright red. "Good. Now straddle him."

"What?"

"Hop-hop!" She pats the comforter next to the corpse. "I'm not asking you to defile him. Unless you're like some of the people in this town and you're pissed off at him and you want some free hits while he's down. All I need you to do is hold these old hands steady." She holds up two, vein-bulging and liver spot-covered claws, although ironically, they're much more steady than his own at the moment.

Obeying her command, Nick climbs up on the bed as Sybil comes close to finishing the vodka. *Is the AC on?* he wonders, a drop of sweat running down his nose. Sybil mutters something, and he's not sure what. Somewhere between her walking in and him getting on the bed, her strange little gemstone has gone from cool to fiery. She holds her hands in front of her chest, her eyes becoming sharper, yet somehow the image of her face blurs. Nick blinks. Are his eyes watering? Are they crossed and he just can't seem to uncross them? Is there a haze rising in the room, rippling the air, looking like the billowing heat rising from a hot parking lot? It's not hay fever season. But he can hardly see the woman, or even hear what she's muttering.

Her hands shake now, as the elbows straighten and she cups one on top of the other and presses them onto Uncle Hank's chest. "Hold them," she commands, and her voice seems to have changed, seems to be altered by some sound engineer, like the ones Nick encounters in the theater department who lower the pitch of the actors, add some reverb, make it sound as though two or three people are talking with the same voice. There is heat resonating from the back of her bony hands, and that can't be a red glow underneath them, there's no way anyone can set a fire just by holding out their hands. And what good would it do for the dead? Is she drunkenly attempting to set the corpse's chest hair on fire? Is this actually a funeral pyre he unwittingly found himself a part of?

Is he a human sacrifice?

"To ferry the dead is a difficult job," says the new voice speaking through Sybil. Nick's hands feel like they're burning. The red has shined completely through her skin, and now it seems he's trying to hold back not just her fingers, but a wildfire. "But it is not a one-way trip."

Smoke pours from her eyes and her nostrils and Nick struggles not to look. His hair is drenched with sweat and his own heart is pounding. A new warmth can be felt, this one rising up from inside of him. For a moment he thinks the concoction he drank just moments before has fully disagreed with his stomach and is now poised to hit the eject button, but his mouth is dry. Too dry, in fact, so much so that now all he can think of is how much he wants to drench that heat with a drink of water. The taste of ash reaches his tongue, but there's no longer any time to wonder at the sensations of his own body. Sybil has begun to pump her hands up and down on Uncle Hank's chest, still muttering in a voice that isn't hers, so low he can't make out any single word. But there's a glow in between her lips, and the smoke detector above the doorway goes off, sounding loudly. This new cacophony has prompted the men outside the room to begin pounding on the door. When did Sybil have time to throw the lock? Does the room even have a lock? Their shouts sound muffled and distant, as though Nick is drowning in a pool and people are calling to him from above the surface.

It's then that Sybil stops muttering. She continues to pump her hands as though performing CPR, and Nick thinks he knows what she's about to do next. She inhales. The breath drawing in expands her lungs to a size that seems at least twice the capacity they should be able to hold, and with the smoke still filling the room, the pendant glowing hot on her chest, her eyes and her mouth and the spot underneath her hands still glowing, and Nick's own mouth tasting ever more prominently like ashes, Sybil stoops down, presses her lips against the mouth of the dead Uncle Hank, and exhales. Only it's not air that fills the dead man's ribcage. It's fire. This strange old witch must also have some dragon in her. The flames pass from mouth to mouth, Uncle Hank's body shuddering as though this is all being done without him being dead. And then the strangest thing of all: despite Sybil having ceased her pumping on Uncle Hank's chest, the sensation of movement continues. She pulls her hands away, but Nick is stiff, jaw dropped at what his just happened. The bald man's heart is beating, and his lungs contract, causing smoke to pour out his mouth. His eyes remain closed, but now he breaths, and now he lives.

The taste of ash subsides. Sybil steps backward, the flame in her eyes and mouth now extinguished, and uses the wall behind her as a brace to gently lower her butt to the carpet. She breaths heavily, and Nick's first inclination is to go to her, to help her to her feet, but when he does, she refuses. "Just let me rest for a moment." She nods at Uncle Hank. "You're a lucky kid. Since you helped him, now he owes you."

There's a sudden realization that washes over Nick. Has this been a baptism of fire? Has all his nervousness and restraint been drained from his being? Despite the heat, what he feels now is a sensation of temperature drop, like someone opened a window to let the breeze cool the sweat on his skin.

"Can I get you something? Water, maybe?"

"Not unless you want steam shooting out of my ears. Literally." She smiles, and her breathing has already started to become steady again. Nick stands and reaches up above the doorway to disable the smoke alarm. He can still hear shouts from outside, but when he makes a move to open the door, Sybil stops him.

"I wouldn't do that," she says. "The doorknob is probably too hot to touch. Just give it a minute." The smoke still lingers, but the temperature feels like it's cooling rapidly.

Back in the living room the atmosphere's a mixture of relief and concern. For the first time that morning, Nick hugs his girlfriend, squeezing her tightly, feeling somewhat weak in the knees. *It's just the alcohol,* he assures himself. Sybil sorts through her handbag, standing by the front door, and anyone in the immediate vicinity watches her with suspicious eyes. Once Nick lets go and Lillie wipes a tear, the old woman approaches.

"Lillie."

Lillie grimaces. "Sybil."

"We're square." She holds out her index finger and traces the outline of a polygon in the air. For half a second, Nick can almost see the line she's just drawn. "No more favors." Now she turns to Nick. "And you. I sure hope you're hot enough to handle this." Even the wind blown in from Sybil slamming the front door seems warm.

He turns to Lillie. "Yeah, so, when I get home it's gonna be, 'Dear diary. You would *not* believe what happened today.'"

"What *did* happen?" Lillie asks.

"Either a miracle or crime against God. Maybe both. Can I ask you how the hell she owes you a favor?"

"Our relationship with December has always been strained, but it's to our mutual advantage that everyone's allowed to move freely around the city, no matter whose territory you're in. Part of Dez's land includes the barrio, and they prefer settling their own problems. A few years back, they had a few, ah, rouges, and neither she nor Sybil were strong enough to drive them out. They asked me. They didn't know they were asking Henry Tamberelli's niece. Always keep in mind that no one in this business works for free."

"Rogues?"

"It's complicated. Ask me again sometime and maybe I'll tell you more about it."

He stands there a moment, still light, like if he turned his head too sharply he wouldn't be able to stop until hitting the floor. "Excuse me," he says, and rushes out the door.

Outside, Sybil has started down the driveway. It seems she walked to get here, but how she got here so fast is a mystery.

"Sybil, wait!" he calls, jogging to catch up. The old lady turns.

"And what does the pet of a niece of wicca I just revived against my better judgment have to say?"

He stops, suddenly unsure of himself. "Um, I was just gonna thank you."

She faces him with her violet eyes, but on her lips a smile spreads.

"I never asked you your name," she says.

"Nick. Nick Zavislack."

She chuckles.

"The girl finds herself a pet with a name just as silly as hers. Tell me, Nick Zavislack. What do you make of your girlfriend's uncle's authority? Do you know why this place is the butt of every Southern

Californian's joke? It's not an accident. It's because he wants it that way! He wants people to stay ignorant of its secrets, its <u>power</u>. If the Inland Empire is truly an empire, then Henry Tanberelli is the emperor. So what say you, Nick Zavislack?"

He shrugs. "Lillie's my girlfriend. I'll just have to be careful. And if her uncle's a mafia don, then that I think means I have some powerful new friends."

"Does it?"

"And not only that, why should I give her up? Life is short, right?"

"Wrong," she states declaratively.

"Wrong? How can you say that after what you just saw? Some of those old-timers think you just prevented a <u>war</u>. How many lives would have been cut short if that had happened?"

"None." And she's firm about it. "There is no such thing as a life too short. Or even a life too long, for that matter. Everyone dies precisely when they're meant to, whether you understand the purpose or not. There are, however, lives too depraved. Answer me this, Nick Zavislack. What action can you perform for the duration that will last longer than your life?"

Nick opens his mouth, then promptly shuts it.

"Life isn't short at all. Even if you die tomorrow, your life will have been the longest thing you ever did. The only thing that will endure is the memory of your life. Consider what you've learned today, Nick Zavislack, and see that your life is remembered for the right reasons."

He watches her waddle away in the morning sunlight wondering just who this person he's dating really is.

KAMELYTA NOOR

Diary of a Food-A-Holic

Summer is almost over, and I was supposed to lose weight, yet my triple-layer tummy fat is happily resting on my thighs. I actually have to sit up straight because the mere thought of one fat resting on another is just unsettling.

I truly hate being fat, and I bitch about being fat all the time. I try hard not to put on weight, but I just can't stop eating. I just love to eat. I love to munch on crap, sweets and chips. I love anything fried: fried chicken, fried fish, fried zucchini, fried potatoes, fried banana, and fried anything.

And I do so love pastries. I could honestly live joyfully in a bakery. A few months ago, I attended a 1920s party, and Coffee Bean and Tea Leaf was there serving their wondrous pastries, muffins, brownies, scones, and all those good stuff. Guess where I was? Exactly. I parked myself next to their table all night, munching one carb after another. I loved it. It was the best night of my life. Who cares about the damn Charleston? I just needed my pastries to make my night.

I think about food a lot, and I mean a *lot*. During a meeting at work today, someone mentioned going to City of Industry to pick up the mail ballots, and without thinking, I said, "Hey, let me go with you. We'll stop for roast duck at Sam Woo. It is the best!" As a Malaysian-American, I have a highly developed palate for this wonderful delicacy, a real treasure in my home country.

However, I realized that my passion for this feast is not shared by my fellow American friends. All 11 pairs of eyes at the table just stared at me, probably thinking, "What the hell is this woman talking about?" My poor friends. They simply don't know what they're missing.

I want to go to Vegas again because of the buffets. Not because of the gorgeous hotels, not because of the shows, not because of the bright lights, and most certainly not because of the gambling. I just want to go to the fabulous buffets. Mongolian beef, crab legs, fried fish, cannelloni and ziti, Crunchy California Roll, anything with cream sauce, prime rib, and shrimps and shrimps. Damn, I am already salivating just thinking about it.

In a way, I am glad that I don't have much money. Because then I would be checking out those restaurants advertised in Inland Empire Magazine, a lot! Haha! The only time I wish I have loads of money is when I see pictures of those sumptuous food. I don't wish for more money when I see purses, or dresses, or shoes. I only wish I have loads of money so I can visit those restaurants, and chow down every single dishes in those pictures. And I will be happy.

But then again, as much as I love food, I am actually quite lazy. I'd rather lay on the sofa watching the Kardashians being stupid than get up and cook. When I have a certain craving, I quickly forget about making it if I don't have the complete ingredients in the pantry. I just change my menu. I am easy. I am not one of those who would actually make a list of ingredients, go to the store to get them, and cook the dish to perfection. Eghh, forget it. Like I said, I would rather sleep.

I do try to cook every once in a while, depending on my level of exhaustion after work. This week, I have made chicken curry, fried anchovies in hot sauce, Indian style fried noodles with shrimp, deep fried trout with sweet and sour sauce, and stir-fry bean sprouts and broccoli with chicken with a dab of chili oil. Simple stuff, because these past few weeks, I have been working hard. I just don't have the time to slave in the kitchen.

Oh, I am also grateful that my husband is not a food glutton like me. Because if he was, I would be triple this size I am now. It is just more fun to eat with someone who enjoys food. It is more exciting to visit restaurants and try new dishes with a partner who loves to indulge like I do. But because my husband is boring and not adventurous, I don't really find it too enticing to go out and try all that scrumptious and delightful and odd looking stuff alone. Oh, well. God is fair, after all!

Damn, I really don't like the feel of my fatty tummy resting on my thighs. I can't even see my feet when I stand up. I can feel my butt growing bigger and wider. These are definite signs that I need to stop eating so much. I really don't like this fat feeling, and I really hate tight clothes. I feel like a wrapped jackfruit. Disgusting.

I want to look good. I want to look slim and pretty. I don't want to get up in the morning to see a face the size of a dinner plate staring at me in the mirror. So I have to stop asking for a double extra dose of that wonderful honey mustard sauce at the Subway in downtown Riverside every time I go there for one of their healthy sandwiches. But then again, maybe I won't.

The Last Race

"Be careful! Don't get into any accidents!" my uncle said, throwing two keys bound by a thick metal ring into my hand. "Watch the brakes, they need to be replaced soon," he added. The old Corvette was beginning to become a money pit, but I was always there to fix it for him.

"Don't worry, the car likes me better than you." I replied, in a semi-cocky attitude, as I backed down the driveway.

The car was a 1984 Corvette with the Z51 suspension package. A large blue racing stripe stretched over the top of the hood, roof and rear trunk lid. It had light weight diamond spoke wheels powder coated in gloss black wrapped in high performance low profile Goodyear Eagle HP tires on it. Twin red, Grand-Sport style, hash mark stripes graced the driver's-side front fender. The best part was the factory removable top. Loosen four latches and the top came completely off, convertible style. The old Cross-Fire Injection engine had a deep raspy sound to it. The suspension was very stiff and rattled your kidneys out on anything but the most perfectly smooth roads. However, that was the price you paid for go-cart like handling.

The radio station forecasted light traffic going into LA with no SIG alerts. My goal was to get there and back before rush hour traffic. The place I was traveling to was a junkyard that specialized in old Corvettes, the largest in the nation. I knew I could find everything I needed there. It was quite a distance from Riverside, but I would enjoy driving there like I did many times before, especially with the top off this time.

I merged onto the freeway and checked the mirrors for other traffic. I flicked the turn signal on and moved into the number 2 lane. Traffic on the westbound 60 was light with no delays. I gave a quick glance down at the instrument panel to look at the various readouts on the liquid crystal display screens. Coolant temperatures were in the 180-185 degree range. The oil pressure was steady and strong. The MPG readout was averaging a steady 25 mpg. Pretty good for a 20 year old sports car, I thought to myself.

I got onto a clear stretch of the freeway and opened it up. Up in the distance, a late 80's Ford Mustang was traveling in the fast lane. I moved over into fast lane and began to keep pace with him. I didn't want to spook the Mustang driver into doing something reckless, so I stayed back a few car lengths. There are just too many cops around these days ready to bust you with a huge speeding ticket fine. I continued to pace the Mustang when I looked down at the instrument cluster. The speedometer was reading a solid 85mph and slowly rising.

All of a sudden, the Mustang driver started to pull away from me, so I increased the throttle to keep up. "This is a Corvette! You can't outrun a Corvette!" I confidently muttered to myself. I continued to increase my speed when I noticed almost 100mph reading on the digital speedometer! The speed kept increasing until I saw 130mph flash on the LCD screen.

"Ha! Is 130 all you got in that thing?" I shouted out loud. I stepped on the throttle and quickly closed the distance and then changed lanes to overtake him. I pulled an instant three car lengths on him and continued to accelerate while the digital speedometer flashed 125, 128, 130, 131, 132, 133....

"Come on baby, let's see 140mph!" I shouted to myself. 134, 137, 138, 139, finally I saw 140 flash on the LCD screen! I looked in the rearview mirror and the Mustang was far behind in the distance. Didn't he have enough power to keep up? Did he chicken out at the last minute? What had happened, I wondered to myself.

When I looked forward again, traffic was beginning to get heavy, so I lightly tapped the brakes to reduce my speed. The brake pedal seemed to be spongy at first, so I pressed the pedal even harder. When I did this, the pedal instantly went to the floor. My uncle had warned me about the brakes, but I didn't know they were this bad.

Before I could react with my right hand to pull up on the emergency brake to help slow the car down, the Corvette skidded into the back of a big rig in the number three lane. The fiberglass sports car disintegrated in a bright flash of exploding fiberglass, metal and plastic. I could feel the shards of broken glass slashing through my face. I could smell the bitter aroma of burning plastic and rubber scorching my lungs. An intense pain overcame my whole body. The ride was over.

The next thing I heard was a voice asking me, "Can you hear me? We're getting help! Don't move! We're calling 911....don't move!"

Daily Trance

Who transports us
Seeping into a new dawn
Before yesterday
Was tomorrow's dreams

My heart bleeds   with beating
Untouched   by surgeon
But thou   Lover
Every diastolic amplitude
A river raft of love

The body world
Is the soul's possession
No need   to repent
But return   to need

Gasps only point time
Toward greater breaths

Tranced with madness
There again
Retrievable only by obsession
The universal insanity

The Creature Call

Dawn and Dusk
Are portent to
High Noon & Dark Moon

Living between worlds
you inhabit neither
. . . and both

As cusping Lybra is heated
by Scorpionic visions
I still the fey night
To dream the daylight

Balance is overthrown
by instinctual callings
Subtle envelopment of
cacooning webs

The owl hoots the music
Desire on the prowl

Stand Down

The misunderstood seem to find understanding,
and understanding gets misunderstood
Kind of a George Bush profundity
when a perfect logic rattles around in the brain
 ' til it ricochets into a puzzle
Like a bullet theory in a dead Kennedy
An enigma is more useful than a solution
Like you and me and a generation of otherwise bastards

Am I understood ___ I'm sorry   I only meant to stand
Apart ___ neither under, nor amiss
Nor upon, yet over and over
Like a recount of ballots or a momentous monetization
Of one and therefore all
As one missed over stood and one stood over didn't miss
And then the understanding and the misunderstanding
Just sat down

The Mission Inn and More

It's funny, the things we remember. Sometimes, you can even re-member the clothes you were wearing at the time of a particular event. It was 1973 and go-go boots and mini skirts were in. I was wearing a red mini-skirt, a white, long-sleeved blouse with sheer puffy sleeves and, of course, my white boots and I was looking for my lawyer's office.

His name was Tom McGrath and he had moved his office to the Mission Inn. He was a large man, with shoulders that were kind of hunched and one lazy looking eye—but he was the kindest, fairest lawyer I have ever met. I hadn't been to the Mission Inn in a while but it seemed right and fit that this man would have his office there.

My Grandma Norton had always loved the Mission Inn. When I was younger, she had taken me there. Memories of childhood can be spotty but there are certain clear, snapshot images that remain in your mind. I remember Grandma and I being in the catacombs and they were a little scary. Seeing the catacombs had given me a glimpse to what it must have been like in the days of dungeons and Inquisitions, the days when Edgar Allen Poe created the horrors of *The Pit and the Pendulum* and *The Cask of Amontillado*. The floors of the catacomb hallways were ce-ment and slanted and it was peopled by religious figures. I could picture the evil Montresor leading Fortunado to his fate through the winding catacombs as they sought the cask of Amontillado.

In 1963, when I was pregnant with my second child, the Mission Inn was thrown wide open and people were able to wander through certain sections. It seemed downtrodden and sad. Over the next few years, if the Inn was open or in business, it seemed as if there was always something in the news about someone pilfering or downright stealing—for example, the chef would be passing expensive cuts of meat out the back door to his cohorts. Some of the Inn's furniture disappeared.

Thus, ten years later, I was glad that something was happening in the Inn, even if it were only my lawyer's office. The mall was quiet, different than the days I remembered going downtown with my grandma, before the mall, when the streets were still open. Back then, downtown was filled with stores and offices—Sears, Montgomery Ward, and Karl's Shoes. There were ladies' clothing stores such as Viva's, Marti's and Kristi's. There was a Newberry's and Woolworth's with a soda fountain—but my favorite to remember was J.C. Penney with its little cable basket that went up to the second floor with your money and returned with your change. My grandma and grandpa went to the upstairs offices of the Doctors Inaba for their dental care. They were of Japanese descent and must have been the cheapest dentists in town or my grandparents wouldn't have gone there. Memories of World War II were still fresh and they were prejudiced—but frugal won out over prejudice.

Now, in 1973, the Inn was in an arrested state of shabbiness and decay. I peer at the sign taped on the door. Lawyers? Fourth floor. The elevator looked creaky and clattery and claustrophobic. I opted for the stairs. Whew! What a climb! Huff, puff. The stairs look crumbly and I don't want to look down as they spiral below me. A lady named Marilyn from the Rubidioux area had jumped to her death from the top of these dizzying stairs. I suppose if one were to take her own life, the Mission Inn would seem to be a good place to end it all, the blood, the memory of fractured bones fading into the history of the place until no one remembers, like Fortunado's in Edgar Allen Poe's story.

At the top of the stairs, I find the door to Mr. McGrath's office. I jiggle the handle which is slow to loosen its grip and open. Its quiet inside, very quiet—but I recognize the furnishings from his previous office. The chairs are orange plastic and seem to be out of place here in the Mission Inn. I pull the drapes aside and look down upon a courtyard. Dainty little lawn chairs, chipped, white wrought iron with round seats—shabby, shabby chic before shabby chic was in—are lined up. I wonder, how long have they been waiting for the party that never came—and how much longer must they wait? How long before the clink of glasses, music and murmurings, the swish and rustle of people in motion, the rattle and clang of the kitchen, the heart, the life, of the Inn returns?

My lawyer enters and welcomes me to his inner office. He wears a tweedy coat and, if we were to add a hat and a magnifying glass, he looks like he could have been Sherlock Holmes in another life. He runs his fingers across the books in his bookshelves until he finds the one he is looking for. Yes, there is an easy answer—an easy legal answer, that is—to complete the divorce I had started a year or more previous. Sometimes legal answers can be found in a book; answers for the heart cannot. He tells me it was the other side of the Inn where Marilyn jumped to her death.

It is time for me to leave and he escorts me to a different door; I see the spiraling stairs to my left, to my right is a long hallway. We talk a bit and I feel a warmth toward him and to the Inn itself. I see a door with the name Dr. M. C. Baldwin painted on it. It's so quiet; I can't imagine patients coming way up here to see a doctor and I wonder, how come Dr. Baldwin has his name on the door and no one is looking for him and my lawyer has somebody looking for him and there's only a little sign taped on the door downstairs?

Years later, my daughter and I are in downtown Riverside and the Mission Inn now has a little café on the Sixth Street side. We really like Simple Simon's but on this day, we choose to eat at the Mission Inn restaurant. She orders some offbeat tomato dish and I must be feeling adventurous because I order the same. A little later, the chef comes out to talk to us; he wanted to see who ordered the tomato dish. Apparently, not too many people did—and today, today! there were two orders for it. He sits down to chat with us. I tell him about my long-ago visit to the lawyer. He is Tom McGrath's son.

JEAN WAGGONER

Riverside Dreamscape

The short, round-faced woman sets down
her animal child
and you, my husband/
my lover, draw me along
in the procession
of god-like saltimbanques

The child, invincible,
chases dogs, cats,
a small frog across the garden
of the abandoned home

as I grab a live, biting
sock monkey the size
of my hand
from its grip on the back screen door
and conscript Lorraine,
other strong bodies

to push found objects –
two huge doors –
along the packed-dirt street;
large khaki-colored
sheets of metal and glass,

some panes shattering
with indelicate movement,
parts of their upright edges bent
like the big, demented Veteran
hefting one end
until the turn,
where rubble and plastic trash
fill roadside ditches

We straddle rusting pipes and rotting boards
while the doors take an
alternate route to the back of
the "new" house

We enter across
a see-through porch of fine-cut 1860
pine, its solid-footing rotted to shaggy
grey slats, spongy to our steps
as we walk softly
into a Victorian
expanse of high
ceilings and wainscoted
parlors, dimly-lit
hallways

a warren of bedrooms,
mattresses on the floor,
an abundance of
blankets, sheets,
inhabitants welcoming
us to explore,
ascend to another floor

In some clan confusion of
who goes where
and talk of preparing food,
parting us,
playing games of
trading faces

I long to find your pallet,
which I do, and
slip myself in,
slide my leg across your thigh,
as real as yesteryear

Yet here we are
standing
in a dusty garden
amid a crowd of changed faces
where you turn, smiling, say,
"Let this meal
be my promise,"

before we are back inside, moving toward
Larry's front room, upstairs,
a kind of den, where my
tall, thin, third brother lies prone,
his violently shaking legs
pinned down by a friend,
another ministering aid with pink-
covered bindings of electrical wire

strange life lines,
the pale pink wires
glow and pulse until
the shaking stops,
someone cries, "He's dead!"
and I wail in protest, "NO!
He can't be!"

-- awakening to find
there has been a stay:

my brother is alive, among us
and I've got these
surrealistic, Artaud blues again.

J. LADD ZORN

Whale Song

"I got me one of those little tape recorders 'cause I hate taking notes, and my boss talks too damn fast, and I was playing with it while I drove down Coast Highway today," Valdes said. "I saw this guy with a duffel bag and his thumb out, and I was coming from mass, so what the hell, I stopped to pick him up, 'cause, you know, I been there. So he gets in and he doesn't say anything and I say, 'Where you heading?'

"He says, 'The equator.'"

"I don't know what to make of that, if he's joking or what, so I just nod, and I don't know what else to say, so I just drive trying to think of something to say that ain't stupid, and it's like this guy, I don't know how to explain it, like the quiet is coming from him. I don't know crud about this guy. I only been around him five minutes, and I'm afraid to say something stupid. He was grave, and you know me, I don't use words like 'grave', but even *I* know 'quiet' ain't enough word for this guy. And it wasn't like he's much older than me, shoot, he mighta been younger. His face looked young, but he had a long beard that was red, but it was full of white, too, especially his sideburns, so I don't know how old he was, but listen to this, man; it's wild."

Valdes put his little tape recorder on the table and pushed play. It hissed and then a voice said, "Mind if I turn on the radio? I've got to get a song out of my head."

"That's him, the hitchhiker," said Valdes.

"Go ahead," I heard Valdes say on the tape. "But the knob's broken, and it's stuck on some university station."

"...however, if evolution is true, if eons ago, sea creatures crawled from the ocean and adapted to land and eventually became mankind, then isn't it conceivable that there are creatures in the ocean today whose ancestors remained in the ocean, yet evolved at the same rate as the creatures which we are now? Why aren't their brains, their thoughts, their modes of communication, as advanced as man's," said a voice on the radio.

Another said, "Clearly, no other species has contributed to technological progress the way man has. That progress would seem to be the measure of species intelligence. Have dolphins developed rockets to the moon? Have whales researched cures for cancer?"

162

"Do they have nuclear missiles? Do they have chemical waste? Do they make smog?" "Hmmmm. Okay, we need to take a break and then we'll be back with marine biologist--" Click. "Right there he turned off the radio with these bony fingers of his," said Valdes. Then on the tape, Valdes said, "Ridiculous, huh?"

The tape hissed a while longer with the sounds of the truck bouncing along. "He kept pulling at that beard of his," Valdes said, "but keep listening. He's gonna start talking in a minute." After a few minutes, the voice of the hitchhiker said, "I spent some time in Alaska with this guy. Ernest Ledger. We spent a couple of seasons with the salmon fleet up there."

"Out the corner of my eye, I could see his face flickering with memory," said Valdes. "I don't know if that's the right word, man, you're the writer, but I say his face was flickering."

Then the voice of the hitcher on the tape said, "Ledger was crazy, but I liked him. Alaska, man, it's beautiful. Up around Barrow, there's a time of year when the sun just hangs there over the horizon moving sideways big and red, and it takes hours to go down, sideways. That's during the summer, during the salmon season. And then there's a twilight that lasts forever; that's fall coming, and the crabbers go out. Slowly it gets dark; takes weeks and weeks to get dark, but it gets cold real quick, and the dark lasts longer and longer until the sun inches up for a little bit and sinks again until it just stops coming. At night, that Aurora Borealis streaks the sky and seeing that, man--Ledger said it drove him crazy.

"It's beautiful, but it's lonely, and they got some scary weirdos on some of those boats. Ledger was cool, though. I liked him because it got really boring sometimes, but he never stopped talking. He had been a theology student, studied comparative religion at Berkeley before he dropped out and answered an ad in the school newspaper about working in Alaska for the summer. We'd be hauling in the empty nets and he would just keep babbling on about all this crazy stuff, about the Eskimo beliefs, the Tlingit spirits, and about demons, and all this stuff. He didn't seem to care whether or not you listened, he would just keep talking. Most of the rest of the crew didn't like him. Some guys thought he was the reason we weren't getting any fish. Our skipper hated him. Knox was his name. Knox thought he was running a prison or something. If you were younger than he was or from farther south than he was, he despised you. And he was always saying things about God punishing mankind for its liberal ways.

"Ledger and me always got the worst jobs. The fishing was really bad that year. The old-timers all talked about how it got harder every year and that this year was the worst of all, and everyone was in a foul mood about there being no fish. No one knew if it was because of warmer temperatures, or El Nino currents or over-fishing or pollution or what, but even the sea lions were starving to death; we'd pull their scrawny carcasses in with our nets, and the skipper just kept getting meaner and meaner. Ernie routinely told him to shove it. One day, near the beginning of summer, Knox caught Ernie and me smoking some stuff we weren't supposed to be smoking. Ernie had snuck some on board, and sometimes on our watch, when the crew was asleep, we'd go astern and have a quick puff."

The hitchhiker made a sound that was a cross between a chuckle and a groan. "That was a big screw up," he said. "The captain just smiled and said something about federal maritime laws and the coast guard and about how we were going to have a nice year in jail when we got back to Dutch Harbor. So that night--and when I say night, I mean about one hour after midnight that it was dark--we took one of the Zodiacs and loaded it up with supplies and rowed until we were far enough away to start the motor. I still can't believe we didn't get caught. We knew they'd look for us to go south, so we went north. We figured we could hide out a few weeks, and everyone would figure we were dead. Ernie said he knew a place we could camp and trap rabbits and maybe even a caribou, and get mushrooms." The hitcher stopped.

"He's lighting a cigarette," said Valdes.

"We motored north until we came to this cove. There're hundreds of coves, but this one had this natural jetty of rocks that hid the entrance from the sea; you'd've had to know it was there to spot it. The beach there is beautiful. Not like here, man. No condos. Just evergreens and rocks and moss. Some of the birds and rabbits up there didn't seem to have learned any fear of humans, and for a little while, they weren't too hard to catch. And whatever was wrong with the fish in the ocean, I don't know, but we kept finding seals too starving to get away, and we'd club 'em and cook 'em. They didn't have much meat, but they had some. We didn't know how long we'd been up there. The sun stopped going down. It seemed to be circling us, going around and around on the horizon, but we couldn't have been that far north. I don't think we were sleeping right. I think my mind was playing tricks. The whole time Ledger was going on and on about how free his soul was, and how he was filled with the spirit of the universe and all this crazy stuff. 'These woods are filled with the spirit, man, I swear to God! I can feel it all around us, man. Dontcha feel it?'" The hitcher's voice rose and fell and cracked.

"We had walked out on that jumble of rocks that arranged themselves out into the ocean like a jetty. It was this gray day. You didn't know where the sun was. You couldn't see the sky or the horizon. We were just lazing there on our backs. The tide was coming in, swelling and surging around us, I swear the rhythm of it affected your thinking. Ledger was going on like usual, 'I swear I understand the trees. They express themselves through their posture; they've been through things that affect who they are. It's all around.' He said it like he said everything, with firm, deep belief. And I don't know, the truth is, I was feeling something. It did seem like the world around us was animated with intelligence, even the rocks seemed to express design. Then Ernie jumped up and pointed. 'Look, man, look! Do you see 'em?' I looked. For a second, I thought we had been caught. A dozen tall sails sliced through the surf, glistening black. Then I figured it out. They were killer whales.

"It was high tide now, and they were swimming all around us, so close, you could have reached off the rocks and touched them. You could tell they knew we were there, and Ernie was getting really excited. 'Oh, man, do you hear 'im?! I swear to God, I hear 'im!' The hitcher's voice rose. 'I understand the whale songs,' Ernie was yelling, and fog was coming out of his mouth. 'They want to meet us,' he was saying, and he started pulling off his boots. 'I'm gonna swim with 'im, man. C'mon!' He sounded so sure. I got up and I go, 'Ernest, I donno, man…It looks pretty cold.' He was unbuckling his pants. 'Dontcha hear 'im? We understand each other, it's all one spirit; they know it, too, man. Don't you?' He was standing there buck naked looking at me like *I* was crazy.

"'You'll freeze,' I said, but I was the one stood there frozen and fascinated and believing in him as he entered the water and swam away from the rocks. The whales swirled around him, those false white eyes staring blankly through the dark water. 'Oh my God!' he screamed. 'This is magnificent!' And he reached out and grabbed a dorsal fin as it went past, and it towed him along. He laughed this mad, joyous laugh. He was coughing and laughing and shrieking, and I was laughing, too. One tossed him exulting through the air. Ernest splashed into the water, and another came and pulled him under. The laughter turned to gurgling and the water turned red. One had him by the legs, and another ripped into his side, pulling him apart. 'Oh, God! Oh God!' he was screaming. The water churned, and then after a while, I just couldn't hear him or see him anymore. I sat back down on the rocks and stayed there who knows how long. I could hear the whales. They were giggling and talking and their voices--they were saying---shit, I don't know, but they were talking to me, you could hear their tone, mocking, and daring, and coaxing, trying to get me to come in the water. I covered my ears and closed my eyes, and still I heard their voices. I can hear them still."

The taped hissed. Valdes didn't say anything.

"Finally, waves began splashing over me. The tide was at its height. I opened my eyes and the whales were circling, and I hugged my legs to my chest and was just rocking there, shivering and I'm not a religious man, but I was praying, praying my ass off that that water wouldn't get any higher. I don't know if I fell asleep or something, but it was like I suddenly opened my eyes and the tide had lowered and the whales were gone. Pins and needles pricked my legs and it was a long time before I was able to walk back over the rocks to the beach."

Here Valdes mumbled something incomprehensible, and then there is a long pause on the tape.

"I done a lot of walking since then," said the hitchhiker. Then he groaned in horror. "I don't expect anybody to believe me, but I gotta tell people." He groaned again. "Will you let me off up here? I gotta put my legs on the ground."

"I pulled over, and he got out," Valdes told me. Then on the tape you hear the hitcher say, "I been on land ever since," and the sound of the door shutting and Valdes mumbling.

He turned off the tape and looked at me for some remark.

"I doubt it," I said.

"Why? You think orcas don't eat people? They would if they were hungry enough. If there are no salmon and no seals…If the food chain is that messed up…"

I couldn't help laughing. "You believe everything, man. You know how I know that guy's full of it? Because his prayers were answered, man. That's when you know for sure you're hearing a fairy tale."

Valdes clucked and swiped his tape recorder off the table. "You know what your problem is? You don't believe nothin'."

"Whatever." I laughed again, but it was joyless and sardonic.

"I gotta go," Valdes said. "I just thought you'd think it was interesting."

I couldn't think of a proper response.

"See ya," he said, and went out the door and shut it.

"I believe I wouldn't be dumb enough to swimming with killer whales in Alaska!" I called to the closed door.

I turned back to my laptop and wrote down everything I just heard, and what's weird is, the thing I took from the whole story is, I'm jealous of Valdes.

Cynthia Anderson is a writer and editor living in Yucca Valley. Her poems have appeared in numerous journals and won awards from the Santa Barbara Arts Council, the Santa Barbara Writers Conference, and the Wildling Art Museum . Her latest book is *In the Mojave* (Pencil Cholla Press, 2011). Her collaborations with photographer Bill Dahl can be seen online at www.rainbear.com. She is co-editor of *A Bird Black As the Sun: California Poets on Crows & Ravens* (Green Poet Press, 2011).

In 2003 **Lee Balan** opened a doorway to an alternate universe and ever since he has been traveling from here to there. His art-constructs and poetry have been inspired by his travels. Lee Balan was the first editor and art director for *Beyond Baroque Magazine* in Venice, CA. His poems and stories have been published in several magazines. His background in mental health has been a major influence on his work. Lee has been the featured poet at several events in the Coachella Valley.

Hong-My Basrai was born and raised in Saigon, Vietnam and has lived in Southern California since 1984. Fluent in Vietnamese and French and a Chemical Engineer by training, Hong-My has dedicated herself to her family, home schooling two of her children until two years ago. Hong-My has been a writer all her life. She is currently pursuing the publication of her memoir, *Behind the Red Curtain*, a harrowing account of her family's seven-year long struggle to regain freedom following the fall of Saigon. She also blogs actively and has written several short stories and poems. A member of two writers' clubs, she is a Board Member of the Writer's Club of Whittier.

Michael Bennett, a writer whose background is in motion picture production, frequently finds himself, as in *Hwy. 62 to Yucca*, living what can best be described as "a scene from a movie". Occasionally he records these experiences as short stories. He is currently trying to find another form in which to share these experiences.

While visiting Palm Springs a decade ago, **Alaina Bixon** became enchanted with the desert landscape and shortly afterwards transplanted herself from San Francisco. She completed her MFA in Creative Writing and Writing for the Performing Arts at UC-Riverside, Palm Desert, with an emphasis on creative nonfiction. She is a freelance writer, teacher and editor, currently working on profiles of local personalities and helping clients with their memoirs. Palm trees still make her giddy.

168

Alissa Bixon was an internist before laying down her stethoscope and picking up a pen and paintbrushes. She is very glad that decisions now are aesthetic, rather than life or death. Although her aesthetic choices often seem pretty life-or-death to her.

Karen Bradford is an award-winning freelance writer/photographer whose clients have ranged from a paleontology and archaeology museum to a cyberspace forensic technologist. Her former career positions include as public relations manager at *The Press-Enterprise*, campus communications officer in business and economics for University of California Riverside and also lecturer in public relations at UCR. Her degrees are in communications: an M.A. in public relations and a B.A. in photojournalism. Her writing and photography have won first place in both national and regional competitions, been published in national magazines and featured in international exhibits. She has volunteered her photojournalism for Rotary International around the world.

Nancy Scott Campbell has been a desert hiker and resident for more than twenty years. She has been a Mediator, has taught English as a Second Language, is a Physical Therapist, and is delighted with the workshops of the Inlandia Institute.

Nikia Chaney is a native of the Inland Empire, with an MFA in Poetry from Antioch University, LA. She has upcoming publishing in *Pearl, Sugar House Review*, and *New York Quarterly*. Nikia is surrounded by very tiny people; she has five of her own, including a three month old baby, and she also teaches a children's poetry class for the Top Flight after school program.

Deenaz P. Coachbuilder, a Riverside, California resident, is a published poet in the U.S. and India, an educator, artist, writer and environmental advocate. She received a Doctorate in Theater, an M.S. in Communicative Disorders in the U.S., and an M.A. in Literature from Bombay University, India. A retired school principal, she is a consulting Speech Pathologist and university professor in "special education." A Fulbright scholar, Deenaz is the recipient of several awards, the most recent being President Obama's 2011 "Volunteer Service Award." Her first book of poems will be published in 2012.

Mike Cluff is a full-time English and Creative Writing instructor at Norco College. His forthcoming book, *Elegant Worry*, is scheduled to be published in late 2011. In his free time, he paints and acts in community theater throughout Southern California.

Avika Dhillon is a thirteen-year-old 8th grade student who enjoys reading, sketching, and writing. Her inspiration for this particular poem came from the Gage Canal.

Dr Harki Dhillon is an Orthopedic Surgeon in Riverside, California. He is the Founder and President of the Riverside International Film Festival, now in its tenth year. He is on the Board of Trustees of University of California Foundation, Riverside, the Board of Advisors of California Baptist University and the Chancellor's Circle of Riverside Community College. He is the Producer of a critically acclaimed Hollywood feature film "Beyond Honor" and an advisor and actor in another feature film "American Blend". Harki's book - *Invisible Hands, A book of poetry* is now available on amazon.com. He is a featured poet in the summer, 2011 issue of *Inlandia: A Literary Journal*, and has been published in *Phantom Seed* and *Slouching towards Mt Rubidoux Manor*. Harki is now working towards completing his memoir.

Heather Dubois writes dark fiction and psychological thrillers. She has a short fantasy piece published in the third issue of Slouching to Mt. Rubidoux Manor, and is finishing up her Fiction Writing Certificate through the UC Riverside Extension Program. She has lived and worked in several areas of the Country but has settled in the Inland Empire, in the foothills of San Bernardino. In memory of her boys Del and Charlie. Miss you both.

Myra Dutton is the author of *Healing Ground: A Visionary Union of Earth and Spirit*, published in 2003 by Ten Speed Press in Berkeley, California. *Healing Ground* was a 2004 Narcissus Book Award finalist for *New Age Retailer Magazine*, and was recognized as 2003's "Top Ten Books" by *Shutterbug Magazine* and 2006's "Ten Books We Love" by *Inland Empire Magazine*. Myra has appeared on PBS and NPR and was a featured poet at Beyond Baroque, Tebot Bach, Moonday Poets, and Inlandia Institute at Riverside Public Library. She has interviewed Billy Collins, Galway Kinnell, Lucille Clifton, and David St. John.

Cyrus Emerson has a BA in journalism from Southern Oregon University. He has written for the *Ashland Daily Tidings*, Jefferson Public Radio, and the Inlandia Institute. He is also the author of two books, *Lost Angel*, and *Fear and Loathing in the State of Jefferson*. Currently, he produces an Arts and Entertainment pod cast available on iTunes called "Get Behind Me, Now Stay There".

Glen Fitch is a 16th Century poet lost in the 21st Century. He was born near Niagara Falls, educated in the Catskills, and offered alternatives to violence to men on the Monterey Bay. Glen now lives with his custom motorcycle designer partner in Palm Springs. Retail, not academics, pays the bills. Someday he will finish Spenser's "The Fairie Queene."

Amy Floyd has been a member of the Inlandia Creative Writing program since its beginning. She has been published in *Slouching Toward Mt. Rubidoux Manor* books 1-3, as well as *Phantom Seed 4*. She self published an e-book entitled *Do Serial Killers Smile At Their Victims?* through Amazon.com last April and is currently in the process of publishing more electronic works. Part time writer, full time mother, she enjoys looking at the world in an unusual way, which spurs her imagination and inspires her to be a better person.

Carissa Garcia was born and raised in the inner city of Fresno, California. She is working on her Bachelor of Arts in World Arts and Cultures at University of California Los Angeles after transferring from Riverside City College and having attended Fresno City College. She has explored various parts of the Mojave Desert where her mother's family has native roots. A poem of hers, "El Camino de Los Ancianos," was published in *Phantom Seed.*

David Calvin Gogerty is an economist whose professional work is for private clients on problems of risk analysis. He is a co-author of articles in peer-reviewed journals in economics and operations research. He and his wife live in a small mountain community in Southern California.

Michelle Gonzalez earned her BA in English from the University of California, Riverside. She also received her teaching credential from University of Phoenix and MFA in Creative Writing from National University. For the past 29 years she has lived in Riverside and has no plans on leaving the Inland Empire. Her poems have been published in National University's literary magazine and other local magazines. Michelle plans to publish her first book of poems soon as well as continuing her teaching career.

Emily Heebner has taught as a part-time adjunct instructor in California for several years. She is a veteran theatre actor whose work has included the national tour of *Noises Off* and stints at Actors Theatre of Louisville, Berkeley Repertory Theater in Berkeley, CA, and South Coast Rep. in Costa Mesa, CA. She holds a BA from Cornell University, an MFA from the American Conservatory Theatre, and an MA in English from California State University Northridge. Her writing has appeared in *The Christian Science Monitor* and the University of Maine's *Binnacle*.

Joan Koerper, (Ph.D. in Humanities), writer, educator, potter and transpersonal psychotherapist, has published creative nonfiction/memoir, poems, fiction and nonfiction in such venues as *Sacred Fire (Adams Media), Moondance, Clay Times, The Single Parent*, newspapers, Inlandia publications, radio and videotape scripts, one of which won honors, audiotape scripts for children and her book, *Singing Over the Bones...* (UMI, 2004). She has written and performed a one-woman play, and her research is housed in libraries. She has taught graduate and undergraduate courses at four universities. Active with Paws for Literacy, she and her dog Sage have just completed their novel *Dumped, Dazed and Dazzled* for young readers.

Noreen Lawlor is a poet and an artist who lives in Joshua Tree with her son and two Yorkies. She loves to write about the Mojave Desert and the wondrous creatures who survive there. Her poem "A loaf of White Bread" was inpired by an assignment given in Maureen Alsop's workshop. Currently, Noreen is working on a project that combines her graphic art and poems. Several of her poems have been published in the *Sun Runner* and on line.

Don Lenik moved to Idyllwild in 1994 with his wife Sheila (now deceased) after he retired from his work in Los Angles as a journeyman pressman. He joined the first Idyllwild Writers Workshop in the summer of 2010 and has been the group's most stalwart member. Besides sharing his writing in workshops, Don keeps loneliness at bay by volunteering and participating in a number of other community groups, most notably the Garden Club, the Idyllwild Chorale, the boosters for the Lemon Lily festival and the Associates of Idyllwild Arts Foundation.

Jan Lucas is a part of the Riverside Inlandia Creative Writing Workshops. This is her first publication. The story, "Michelle Swims with Gold", takes place when her daughter was a child; "The School Bus" is a story based on an actual event that took place during her years as a school bus driver.

172

Marc Lombardo is a fiction writer and poet who lives in Los Angeles, but has spent of a lot of time in Riverside, where he enjoys being a member of the Inlandia Writers Workshop.

Jacqueline Mantz Rodriguez was born in Great Falls, Montana but immigrated to the Inland Empire as a young child growing up in Ontario, California. She resides in Rancho Mirage and works as a special education teacher for Palm Springs High. She is working on her collection of short stories and poetry while preparing a documentary on her special education students. Jacqueline received her B.A. in literature and creative writing from Cal State San Bernardino and her Masters degree and teaching credentials from National University. Jacqueline's loves are her new husband Joe and her Boston Terrier Elizabeth Barrett Browning.

Juanita Mantz grew up in the Inland Empire with her two sisters in a family that memoirs are made of. After dropping out of high school and taking her GED, Juanita waitressed her way though junior college at Mt. SAC and in 1999, she graduated from UCR magna cum laude with a degree in English Literature. In 2002, she graduated from USC Law and worked at large law firms in Texas and San Francisco. After her father died suddenly, she moved back home to the Inland Empire and eventually found her bliss as an attorney with the Law Offices of the Public Defender. She has attended the Inlandia and VONA San Francisco writing workshops and blogs regularly at blogspot.com ("Life of JEM: my life in the Inland Empire"). Juanita is currently working on her memoir "My Inland Empire: Hometown Stories".

Richard M. Mozeleski is a retired Landscape Designer. He has been married to his wife Diane for 22 years, and is the father of Ian Mozeleski, a college Basketball player. Richard has coached local Basketball and Baseball players for the past decade and has recently taken up writing and theatre after moving to the picturesque town of Idyllwild, CA. Richard has recently begun a ministry to feed local homeless men.

Lorraine Naggi earned her BA in English and Creative Writing as well as her credential to teach English from Cal State San Bernardino. She has lived in and around Corona, Riverside, Mira Loma, and San Bernardino for the majority of her life. She wants a full time teaching job, but at this point, any job will do. Previous works include "Crossing the Threshold," "But I Believe in Peace, Bitch," and "Go F*** Yourself, Cinderella." She is married to Peter Naggi and though she didn't wear combat boots underneath her dress, she did headbang and pogo at her reception. To contact her, email at lefaivrl@gmail.com.

Peter Naggi (naw-jee) is wondering just why we put up with calling it the "Inland Empire," so the included story reflects this. His previous works includes Alt_and A Single Second (among others), both appearing in previous volumes of Slouching. Be on the lookout for books in the future, despite his overt lack of publishers or literary representation (and by the way, if you know either, pass the word along). He can be reached at mrarmageddon99@gmail.com.

Kamelyta Noor simply enjoys writing. She enjoys telling the stories of her life, which she thinks is quite interesting. Hah! But most importantly, many many fortune tellers saw in their crystal balls that she is going to be a successful, well known, and rich writer soon. So while waiting for that prophecy to come true, she writes.

Christina Lee Nordella is the creator and owner of Mother Earth Healing Products and President of the EarthWitness Foundation. She is also the first white woman to hike the Lohardi trail in India. Christina works also as a Jin Shin Jyutsu practitioner, Reiki Master and Shamanic healer. She has studied and practiced energy work for fourteen years. She is the author of the poetry book, Broken Open, which she wrote for her family and friends as a gift. Currently, she is finishing a second poetry book that will also include songs. She is a guitar player and belly dancer and lives with her three children in the small community of Idyllwild, Ca.

Joy Sikorski, M.A., an award-winning film composer, performer and educator, founded SingBabySing® and Singing Mastermind™. She received a National Public Relations Society Award for documentary film music, co-composed music and lyrics for *Gathering Blue*, a musical adaptation of Newbery Award-winning author Lois Lowry's book, co-founded an award-winning environmental awareness contest featured on ABC's *Good Morning America*, has appeared on television, been a featured writer in the *Los Angeles Family Magazine*, and created, *Impropera: Music of the Moment*, a unique performance genre. Her current projects include an online singing course, *Fearless Voice Power™*, and several books and original music projects.

Mike Sleboda is a member of the Inlandia Creative Writing program since 2009 and has been published in *Slouching Towards Mt. Rubidoux Manor*. He is currently a volunteer for the Inlandia Institute and earned his B.A. degree in Communications from Cal State University San Bernardino. He plans to pursue a career in TV/film production.

Steve Vaughn is a professional jazz saxophonist, who has played at many bars, parties, and other places throughout the Inland Empire and beyond during his multi-decade career performing solo and with bands. One of his recent performances was for the Inlandia Writers-Riverside workshop showcase in September, 2010 at Back to the Grind Coffee House. He writes poetry and essays that convey the essence of his life as a musician, and lives in San Bernardino.

Mae Wagner sees Inlandia stories everywhere just waiting to be told. She has written for the Riverside Chamber of Commerce, The Chino Champion and had several columns published in the Op-Ed page of the Press-Enterprise when it was locally owned. She currently writes a column for her home town newspaper in Hettinger , North Dakota, even though she has lived in the Inland Empire since 1957. She is a mother, grandmother and great-grandmother and lives in Redlands with her husband, Alex, and her dog, Sophie.

Jean Waggoner established Idyllwild's Inlandia Writing Workshop in the summer of 2010. A "freeway flier" with a Master's from CSU Fullerton, Jean teaches English and ESL at community colleges in Riverside County. Her work includes story-telling, essays, fine arts reviews, advertising copy and poetry that has appeared in on-line and print publications, including business journals, the National Poetry Anthology, Phantom Seed and Inlandia publications. She has read poetry at Inlandia and Idyllwild community events and at the Poetry Week in San Miguel de Allende, Guanajuato, Mx. (Jan. 2009). Jean recently co-authored with Douglas Snow *The Freeway Flier and the Life of the Mind* (ISBN # 978-1-4568-3119-6 paperback, with e-book available at Amazon, soon).

J. Ladd Zorn lives, works, and writes prose and poetry in the Inland Empire, and enjoys making excursions to outdoors places there, in the local deserts, and in the Sierra Nevada. He is currently at work on a novel.

The Inlandia Institute is a regional non-profit literary center. We seek to bring focus to the richness of the literary enterprise that has existed in this region for ages. The mission of the Inlandia Institute is to recognize, support and expand literary activity in all of its forms through community programs in the Inland Empire, thereby deepening people's awareness, understanding, and appreciation of this unique, complex and creatively vibrant region.

The Institute publishes high quality regional writing in print and electronic form including books published in partnership with Heyday under the Inlandia Institute imprint as well as: *Writing From Inlandia: Work of the Inlandia Creative Writing Workshops*; the online literary journal, *Inlandia: A Literary Journey; and*, starting the winter of 2011, books directly under the Inandia imprint, including *A Tale of Two Chilies*, a children's chapter book by Julianna Cruz.

Inlandia presents free public literary programming featuring authors who live in, work in, and/or write about Inland Southern California. We also provide Creative Literacy Programs for children and youth and hold creative writing workshops for teens and adults.

To learn more about the Inlandia Institute please visit our website at InlandiaInstitute.org.

OTHER INLANDIA PUBLICATIONS

INLANDIA ELECTRONIC PUBLICATIONS

Inlandia: A Literary Journey, an on-line journal
Edited by Cati Porter

Expected Winter of 2011
Audio Guide
Inlandia: A Literary Journey Through California's Inland Empire
Moderated by Gayle Brandeis

OTHER INLANDIA IMPRINT PUBLICATIONS

Expected Winter 2011
Tale of Two Chilies
Julianna Cruz

INLANDIA IMPRINT BOOKS FROM HEYDAY

Backyard Birds of the Inland Empire
Sheila N. Kee

Dream Street
Douglas F. McCulloh,
forward by D.J. Waldie

Inlandia:A Literary Journey Through California's Inland Empire
Edited by Gay Wattawa, introduction by Susan Straight

No Place for a Puritan: The Literature of California's Deserts
Edited by Ruth Nolan

Expected in winter 2012
Rose Hill
Carlos Cortez

www.ingramcontent.com/pod-product-compliance
Lightning Source LLC
Chambersburg PA
CBHW051830090426
42736CB00011B/1728

* 9 7 8 0 9 8 3 9 5 7 5 1 5 *